# The Little

# **ACT**

# Workbook

An Introduction to Acceptance and Commitment Therapy: a mindfulness-based guide for leading a full and meaningful life

## Dr Michael Sinclair &
## Dr Matthew Beadman

**crimson**

First edition published in Great Britain in 2016 by Crimson Publishing Ltd
This reprint first published in Great Britain in 2021 by Crimson
An imprint of Hodder & Stoughton
An Hachette UK company

4

A CIP catalogue record for this title is available from the British Library

Paperback ISBN 978 178059 243 5

Printed and bound in Great Britain by Clays Ltd, Elcograf S.p.A.

Hodder & Stoughton policy is to use papers that are natural, renewable
and recyclable products and made from wood grown in sustainable
forests. The logging and manufacturing processes are expected to
conform to the environmental regulations of the country of origin.

Hodder & Stoughton Ltd
Carmelite House
50 Victoria Embankment
London EC4Y 0DZ

www.hodder.co.uk

# Contents

*This little book packs a big punch. You can use it as either a rapid refresher course or a brief but powerful introduction to ACT. With an engaging and easy-to-read style, Mike Sinclair and Matt Beadman take you step-by-step through the theory and practice of Acceptance and Commitment Therapy, and show you how to enrich and enhance your sessions with the core ACT processes. You'll learn how to wake up, loosen up and step up to create a richer, fuller, more meaningful life. An excellent addition to your ACT library.*

**Dr Russ Harris**
**Author of *ACT Made Simple* and *The Happiness Trap***

The Little ACT Workbook *is one of the clearest and best-written presentations of ACT I've seen. Short and practical, you can put it in your pocket and begin immediately to relate to your own life in a new way. Highly recommended.*

**Steven C. Hayes**
**Co-developer of Acceptance and Commitment Therapy, and**
**author of *Get Out of Your Mind and Into Your Life***

The Little ACT Workbook *is a wonderful introduction to how to succeed in life. Based on clear scientific principles and evidence, it may surprise, intrigue, amuse or inspire. It will ask you to look at your circumstance in an entirely different way than you have done before. What you will see is that our goals and our difficulties are connected, our own thoughts are as likely to help as to mislead, and one sure way to lose is to refuse to participate. What you will do is up to you.*

**Lance M. McCracken, PhD**
**Professor of Behavioural Medicine, King's College London**

The Little ACT Workbook *by Michael Sinclair and Matthew Beadman is an excellent introduction to how Acceptance and Commitment Therapy (ACT) can help you to pursue a life of meaning and purpose. The authors have brilliantly distilled the essence of ACT, drawing upon the most up-to-date science that underpins this new approach to cognitive behavioural therapy. This is a clear, engaging guide as to why we struggle with unwanted thoughts and feelings, and what steps you can take for an alternate, effective approach to life's experiences. The book uses carefully chosen exercises and metaphors that will strengthen your ability to be aware of and, most importantly, do what most matters to you.*

**Dr Eric Morris**
**Director of the La Trobe University Psychology Clinic, Melbourne**
**Australia, and co-author of *ACTivate Your Life***

*Want to learn how to get unstuck and get moving in life? Dr Michael Sinclair and Dr Matthew Beadman have written an accessible, fun and practical book that will open you up to the skills to do just that. They artfully bring together the key components of Acceptance and Commitment Therapy, a powerful and scientifically grounded mindfulness-based behavioural change programme. I would highly recommend this book.*

**Dr Joe Oliver**
**Co-author of *ACTivate Your Life***

*I just loved reading this book. It is so practical in its' organisation and written in everyday language that is easy to understand. The authors systematically teach three core ideas which are at the heart of ACT: wake up, loosen up and step up. In each section, they provide numerous, easy-to-follow daily strategies to help increase your ability to be in the present moment, to practise detachment when you are in troubled waters, and to live your life guided by what really matters to you. The case examples used to highlight key concepts are really well done. The authors have succeeded at their goal of making ACT refreshingly simple to understand and utilise in daily life.*

**Kirk Strosahl, PhD**
**Co-founder of Acceptance and Commitment Therapy, and author of *In This Moment: Five Steps to Transcending Stress Using Mindfulness and Neuroscience***

# About the authors

**Dr Michael Sinclair CPsychol CSci AFBPsS** is a Consultant Counselling Psychologist registered with the Health and Care Professions Council, UK. He is an Associate Fellow of the British Psychological Society (BPS), a Chartered Scientist registered with the Science Council and a Senior Practitioner on the Register of Psychologists Specialising in Psychotherapy (BPS). Following several years working within the NHS, Michael now works as the Clinical Director of City Psychology Group (CPG) in London. He is an experienced ACT practitioner who has delivered the highest quality psychological treatment and training for over 16 years. Michael provides ACT interventions to people of all ages, couples and families, who are experiencing a range of psychological problems such as depression and anxiety. He provides ACT coaching to corporate executives, as well as ACT supervision to other psychologists. Michael has published a range of mindfulness-based self-help books, as well as academic papers on his research and practice. He is committed to helping people to live full and meaningful lives.

**Dr Matthew Beadman CPsychol** is a Clinical Psychologist accredited by the British Psychological Society and registered with the Health and Care Professions Council, UK. He works as a Clinical Associate at City Psychology Group (CPG) in London. He has a keen interest and expertise in applying ACT for pain management and is also employed as a Clinical Psychologist within the NHS. Matthew has published peer-reviewed research in a number of clinical areas, written reviews of the evidence supporting ACT interventions, and published experimental research exploring core ACT processes. Matthew has worked as a psychologist in the NHS and prison service for over ten years and is particularly interested in delivering brief, practical interventions, which create meaningful change for his clients within a shorter period of time.

# Acknowledgements

Thank you to our 'nearest and dearest' (you know who you are!) and all our colleagues for their support and patience while we have written this book. We'd also like to thank all the people we have had the pleasure to meet and serve in our work over the years. We are deeply grateful to you for sharing your experiences and a part of your life with us; without you this book would not have been possible. Lastly, but by no means least, we want to express our deepest gratitude to the entire Association for Contextual Behavioural Science (ACBS); we are extremely lucky to be part of such an inspiring community.

# Introduction

Hello, and a sincere and warm welcome from both of us.

We are delighted that you have chosen to read this book and, whatever your reasons for choosing it, we hope it offers you what you're looking for. Perhaps you have already heard of *Acceptance and Commitment Therapy* and would like to find out more about it and how it could help. Or, maybe you have been recommended this book by someone and know very little about Acceptance and Commitment Therapy. Perhaps you are like many other people who have already worked their way through a long list of self-help books and therapies that have advised you to think positively, stop worrying and pull yourself together, in the hope of finding some sense of enduring happiness (if only it was that easy!). Whatever your reasons, the fact that you're reading this book suggests other approaches haven't been as helpful as you were hoping and there is perhaps still something in your life that you would like to change. So, let's take a look at what that might be. How's life going for you? See whether any of the following questions resonate with you.

Perhaps ...

- you've been through a difficult time and you're trying to recover

- you've been struggling to find a sense of meaning, purpose, enjoyment or fulfilment in your life

- you're feeling dissatisfied at work and/or in relationships with friends, your partner or family

- you're feeling a general sense of unease, as if something is missing

- you've been feeling distracted or preoccupied by worries or other repetitive, troubling thoughts or memories

- your life seems controlled by anxiety and a host of associated unpleasant physical sensations

- anger, sadness, fear or other strong emotions seem more in charge of your life than you are

- you notice yourself spending less and less time each day doing the things that really matter to you

- you're lacking the motivation, energy or enthusiasm to get stuck into an aspect of life in the same way that you used to.

Regardless of whether any of these dilemmas or other concerns seem relevant to you, we do hope that this book will be helpful. We also want to assure you that you are certainly not alone in experiencing these kinds of difficulties.

## You are not alone

In Britain today, one in six of the adults you walk past in the street, chat to at work or sit beside on the train are struggling with their emotions to the extent that they would meet diagnostic criteria for a psychological disorder. An even greater number of people will be struggling with other forms of psychological distress. The same is true for people living in the USA and other European countries. In Western nations, up to 40% of all illness is accounted for by mental health difficulties. An astonishing statistic is that twice as many people are affected by these difficulties than by diabetes, heart disease, strokes, cancer and lung disease combined. Now, the vast majority of people who suffer from *physical* health problems will receive treatment. Yet two-thirds of people with *mental* health problems, the most common being anxiety and depression, will not. This is unfair and represents an important form of discrimination. It is particularly sad because many effective, evidence-based psychological treatments exist for those who need them.

## Help is at hand

This book aims to introduce you to a relatively recent and ground-breaking psychological approach that has already been shown by a great deal of scientific evidence to help people to recover from mental health difficulties and to reclaim the life they want to live. This psychological approach is called *Acceptance and Commitment Therapy* and was developed in the USA by Steven Hayes, Kelly Wilson and Kirk Strosahl. Acceptance and Commitment Therapy is often called *ACT*, which is pronounced as one word – 'act' – rather than as the initials A-C-T.

At this early stage it is important to emphasise that ACT is not just a treatment for those who may be experiencing mental health difficulties; the benefits of ACT are far greater and further reaching than that. ACT has the potential to offer each and every one of us a profound insight into the daily stresses and struggles we will all inevitably experience from time to time, as well as a set of invaluable life skills to help us live a more meaningful and fulfilling life. The ideas in ACT are relevant to us all, whoever we are! We know this from the rapidly growing body of research, from our experience of working as Practitioner Psychologists using ACT with clients of all ages, and from our personal experience of applying ACT in our everyday lives.

ACT starts from the idea that when we are suffering in some way, this doesn't indicate that some aspect of ourselves is 'broken' or sick, rather that we've become stuck and caught up in the very natural pitfalls and traps that can affect any one of us. ACT is therefore concerned with understanding the principles and processes that are involved in making us human. In doing so, ACT helps to promote our *psychological flexibility* (a term we will come back to later on), which can help us to make better life choices and ultimately create a life that is rich, full and meaningful.

## Backed up by science

ACT has been developed from laboratory studies of how humans learn to use language and thought, and, at the time of writing, has been tested in over 150 randomised controlled trials. Randomised controlled trials are the same kind of high-quality clinical research trials that are used to evaluate other forms of treatment, such as medication. The results have consistently found that ACT is an effective psychological approach for helping people with an array of common mental health difficulties and other psychological problems, such as depression, anxiety, psychosis, substance misuse and insomnia, and in the management of long-term physical health conditions. ACT has also been shown to help people quit smoking, change their eating behaviour, manage their weight, reduce work-related stress and increase productivity at work. This is a really important point to emphasise; as we just mentioned, ACT is not just for people who are experiencing mental health difficulties. The fundamental principles and techniques of ACT can be used by everyone to help us all *live better lives* – the kind of life we would choose to have.

Having highlighted the evidence supporting ACT, we are certainly not claiming that ACT is the 'right' or best approach to help all people who are suffering, nor that you will necessarily find all the answers to your problems by applying ACT to your life. We are all unique, and different approaches work differently for different people – this is entirely normal. All we can say is that ACT has worked for us personally, and has also worked well for many of the people we have met in helping them to suffer less and to move towards living the kind of life they really want to live. We hope that ACT and the ideas and techniques in this book will help you, too. Of course, you will be the best person to judge whether they do or not through your own personal experience.

## How to use this book

First and foremost this book is intended to be a simple, practical and concise introduction to Acceptance and Commitment Therapy. It is important to emphasise that this book cannot replace the benefits of actually meeting face-to-face with a psychologist or other therapist. This book has not been subject to scientific evaluation, it is merely an introduction to a psychological approach that has been. Furthermore, most psychologists concur with overwhelming evidence indicating that a positive relationship with a therapist who listens to you, who you get on well with and who you feel able to confide in is one of the most powerful ingredients for helping people to make changes in their lives. Needless to say, this book cannot provide this. Instead, we hope that this book might be helpful to you in one or more of the following ways:

■ a an introduction to Acceptance and Commitment Therapy (ACT) and to explain how ACT might help you to make the changes in your life that you hope for

■ by providing an opportunity for you to try out some alternative and revolutionary techniques and strategies designed to help you manage your thoughts and emotions more effectively

- by helping you decide whether you would like to work with a psychologist/therapist who uses ACT

- by providing an alternative source of information and self-help for you to use alongside your work with a psychologist or other therapist who uses ACT.

It's important to emphasise that we have written this book assuming that you have not encountered ACT before, so for anyone entirely new to ACT this is a good place to start. However, if you have read other ACT books or discussed ACT already with a friend or psychologist/therapist and are familiar with the model, we hope this book will still provide a useful refresher as well as giving you lots of opportunities to practise using some key tools and exercises.

As you read this book, we are very keen for you to get your own direct experience of applying ACT. What do we mean by this? Well, we hope that you won't just *read* about ACT but you'll also experience its impact for yourself. This is because (as we hope you will soon discover) ACT is not just an intellectual approach, simply requiring you to engage your head and think your way out of the problems you may be experiencing. Instead, it is a highly experiential approach and about 'getting out of your head' a lot of the time. As you'll see, language and thought can all too often be *the problem* at times, rather than the solution. So, in order to really benefit from ACT, you have to *do it* rather than simply read about it.

Therefore, to ensure that you get a *real feel* for ACT, we've included a number of **experiential exercises** so that you can experiment with using some of these new ideas for yourself. Along with these, you will notice other invitations to try out **specific practical techniques and tasks** designed to help you reflect on the principles and processes of ACT. Some of these tasks will invite you to jot down some notes as you do them; so, if you are reading this electronically, you might like to have a pen and paper to hand, or alternatively you may prefer to use the 'Notes' function on your mobile phone, tablet or other digital device. We have also included a number of **mini case studies**, which have been adapted directly from our work with our clients. Please note that all case study material used in this book has been anonymised to protect the confidentiality of our clients.

We understand that when you come across an exercise in a book like this, it can be very easy to skip it and continue reading. Your mind might give you a million and one reasons why you can't/

won't do the exercise, such as *'I don't have time for this right now'*, *'I don't need to do that'* or *'I'll come back to this later'*. Unfortunately, by listening to your mind and skipping exercises in this way, you may well be missing out on an important opportunity. As we just mentioned, much of the work in this book will be 'experiential'; this means we might ask you to take part in a particular exercise, to remember a particular experience, or experiment with a new idea or metaphor. We do this deliberately so you can experience using ACT, rather than just reading about it.

Learning to use the ideas in this book is a bit like learning to ride a bike; you can read for hours on end about how to balance, steer and push down on the pedals, but you are unlikely to learn a great deal until you actually start trying to ride the bike (and probably fall off a few times!). A similar approach is called for with this book. We try to remind you of this important point with the following bicycle symbol, which you'll find placed next to each exercise throughout the book:

If you're with us on this (which we really hope you are), and you notice that your mind evaluates these exercises as silly or unnecessary at times, we hope that you will *never mind your mind* and instead give ALL these exercises a go as they crop up throughout the book. We want to assure you that we wouldn't invite you to take part in any exercise unless we thought it might be helpful – so, if you're willing to try something completely different, please read on!

## How much time will this take?

Given the brief nature of this book, it might be tempting to read it very quickly in one or two sittings. On the other hand, you might be someone who prefers to work through new ideas like these in a more steady fashion, pausing as you go. It's difficult for us to suggest how quickly or slowly you should read through this book, but our advice would be to give yourself plenty of time to practise and reflect on the exercises and the new ideas. There will also be some exercises that might benefit from a few days or weeks of practice, and some that you might want to return to and repeat. Whatever your approach, we recommend you use this book in a flexible fashion in whatever way seems to work for you, allowing yourself plenty of time to experience the exercises.

## One last important note before we continue ...

While writing this book we've tried our best to include the essential features of the ACT model and to draw upon its core components. We hope the result is a user-friendly, focused, brief and concise guide to the principles and philosophies of ACT that have been so helpful to our clients and us. If you're anything like us, and most of the people we've worked with, you'll also know how life can feel pretty busy and that time often feels very limited indeed. However, this is no reason to miss out on the powerful ideas ACT has to offer. We hope that as you read *The Little ACT Workbook* you will find that there is nothing 'little' about ACT at all, but that this title simply reflects our ambition to create a no-nonsense, straight-to-the-point and bite-size introduction to some really big and important ideas. There are of course some excellent, longer and more in-depth books on ACT, some of which we have listed for you in the 'Recommended reading' section at the end of this book.

We hope you enjoy working your way through this book and that it makes a real difference to your life.

# 1 So what's new about ACT?

ACT derives from a family of psychological therapies called Cognitive Behavioural Therapy, or 'CBT' as it is more commonly known. In its *traditional* format, CBT is currently one of the most widely practised methods of psychological therapy. Backed up by a large body of scientific research, traditional CBT has proven to be highly effective in helping people to manage and overcome a vast range of mental health difficulties and psychological problems. ACT differs from traditional CBT in a number of important ways. Possibly the most significant of these differences is the alternative mechanisms it has at its core in helping people to bring about change in their lives. Rather than necessarily always trying to change or control distressing experiences, such as troublesome thoughts or unwanted emotions (as traditional CBT might advocate), ACT offers an alternative and sometimes more helpful approach. We've often heard from people how, at times, they can feel increasingly stuck and thwarted in their attempts to change, control or distract themselves away from painful thoughts and feelings. When you think about it, you may be able to relate to this. When you've been through difficult experiences in life, how easy has it been to change or control how you've thought or felt about these experiences? It can prove to be a real challenge to try to think or feel differently when life takes a turn for the worse. What's more, recent research indicates that we don't necessarily have to *change* how we think and feel about a situation before we can move on, recover and continue with our lives. This is where ACT comes in – much more on this in the next chapter.

## Getting unstuck and back on track

This book, and ACT, is all about *getting unstuck* and learning new and, hopefully, more effective strategies to handle difficult thoughts, unpleasant emotions and physical sensations when they show up, so that you can *stay on track*. By 'staying on track' we mean doing the things that matter to you in your life and behaving in a manner that's consistent with the kind of person you really want to be – rather than always being controlled by the thoughts, emotions and physical sensations you might experience in any given moment.

Let's take a closer look at what we mean by this. Usually when people pick up a book like this they are hoping to learn some strategies for reducing unwanted thoughts, emotions or physical symptoms – we can think of these as *the problem*. When the problem shows up, people often respond in a fairly automatic and understandable fashion, with certain behaviours designed to make the problem go away. Take Lisa's case, for example.

At 35 years old, Lisa had always been a pretty confident person. However, after a difficult relationship break-up with her now ex-partner, she noticed she had begun to feel more anxious and worried, particularly when socialising with friends and also when speaking up in meetings at work. Now, as Lisa had never really experienced these unpleasant thoughts and feelings before she quite understandably labelled them as *the problem* and responded to them in a completely understandable way – she started doing things to avoid these anxiety-provoking situations. She stopped going to meetings at work, and called in sick or blocked her diary by booking other appointments. Lisa also found that she would avoid making arrangements with friends, and tended to stay at home instead, distracting herself from her worries by watching TV, all in an attempt to feel better and not become anxious. When she felt compelled to attend her best friend's wedding, she noticed how she drank more alcohol than she would normally want to, again in an attempt to reduce her nerves and *control the problem* as she saw it. Although these strategies seemed to be working in the short term by reducing her immediate worries and anxious feelings, they didn't seem to be helping her to eliminate these feelings in the longer term; she still felt anxious about socialising, and at work these feelings just kept coming back. Moreover, Lisa didn't recognise herself any more. She was drinking more than she would like to and had stopped looking after her health. Before, she had really enjoyed socialising and had considered herself an active, supportive team member at work. Although Lisa's coping strategies seemed to help her to curb her anxieties (in the short term, anyway), they certainly weren't helping her to live the kind of life that really mattered to her in the longer term. As a result, she started to feel even more anxious and fed up.

Even at this early stage, maybe you're aware of some of the things you might do when your *problems* show up? Like Lisa, can you spot yourself doing anything to try to control, reduce or avoid your unwanted thoughts, emotions or physical sensations in your life? We'll come back to this in more detail in the next chapter.

## Switching perspective on the problem

If you're like most of us (which we're sure you are!), you can probably notice yourself doing things to try to control, avoid, get rid of or escape from the problems you've been experiencing. Maybe you've been trying to work the problem out; thinking and analysing your way through it for a while and not really getting anywhere?

As we'll discuss in the next chapter, this problem-solving approach to unwanted thoughts and emotions is completely understandable, and similar to the approach we take to physical health problems. For example, if you've got an ache, pain or illness, you go to your doctor or hospital and hopefully there will be medical treatments that can help get rid of the problem.

Similarly, when it comes to psychological problems, sometimes trying to avoid or control our difficult thoughts and emotions can work just fine and have no other consequences – in which case, we don't want to make any changes. For example, someone who lives in England can usually avoid snakes (which can make many of us feel very anxious), and this avoidance has no real costs in terms of quality of life. Sometimes though, these strategies can cause more problems. In Lisa's case, avoiding anxiety-provoking situations and relying on alcohol to help her get through parties may have some unwanted consequences.

All this begs the big question: what is the real problem here? Is it the unpleasant thoughts, emotions and physical sensations – as we tend to assume? Or is it more about our behaviours and responses to these psychological experiences? What do you think?

Unfortunately, when we work hard to avoid or control unwanted thoughts and emotions, life can start to feel like a tug of war with these psychological experiences – the more we try to pull back against them the harder they pull in return – and this can leave us completely *stuck*. Life starts to shrink; it becomes unfulfilling and less meaningful as we end up doing less and less of the kinds of things that matter to us the most.

Again, maybe you can think right now about the ways you have tried to get rid of your problems. Do these strategies really work for you? Maybe they help you feel better in the short term, but what are the longer-term consequences? Do they get in the way of the life that you would prefer to be living? If your answer to this question is 'Yes', then the ultimate question to ask yourself is:

*Would you be willing to respond differently to these problems when they show up, in the service of living an enjoyable, fuller and more meaningful life?*

We ask you these questions, firstly, because they are so fundamental to ACT; and, secondly, because research actually tells us that when people believe they need to try to *control* or *get rid of* a psychological problem before they can continue living their life, this approach generally doesn't work so well and can lead to people becoming even more stuck. If you can relate to this, then we assure you that you're certainly not alone and it doesn't mean that you are 'broken' or wrong in any way – it means you're human! We all do it! But there are times when it is precisely this strategy that keeps the problem going.

If any of this is sounding unclear or confusing right now, that's perfectly understandable. There's no need to try too hard to work any of it out. It will all become clear in time, as we'll be returning to this fundamental principle frequently. In the next chapter we will actually be taking a much closer look at this again and thinking about how we can help ourselves get out of this trap when we find ourselves in it.

## Doing what works

Throughout this book we will be encouraging you to look closely at your *habitual ways of responding* to unwanted thoughts, difficult emotions and uncomfortable sensations and to consider whether these responses are truly working for you; in other words, are they really helping you to stay on track and move towards the kind of life you want to have, or not? We will be asking you to spend some time thinking very carefully about what matters to you most, and what you would choose for your life to be about. You can then consciously use these fundamentally important ideas as a kind of beacon towards which everything else that you do is directed. When the way you respond to difficult thoughts and unwanted feelings moves you towards that beacon, keep going! When your ways of responding move you away from what's important, this book will offer you some alternative ways of responding more effectively to these thoughts and feelings.

## Getting flexible

As we mentioned earlier, ACT is geared towards helping us to increase our psychological flexibility. In essence, this means helping us to get unstuck and to respond more effectively to unwanted thoughts and feelings in the interests of living an enjoyable, fuller and more meaningful life. ACT offers us an array of very helpful and accessible techniques to increase our psychological flexibility. These skills and tools are designed to help us to develop and strengthen (1) *acceptance* (the 'A' in ACT) of difficult experiences, when struggling with these unpleasant experiences stops us getting to where we want to get to; and (2) *commitment* (the 'C' in ACT) to behaving in ways that move us towards the life that really matters to us. There are, in fact, six essential sub-processes that make up the ACT model. However, in this book we have collapsed these down into three key processes for you: **wake up**, **loosen up**, **step up**. This book will help you to develop and strengthen the fundamental principles of Acceptance and Commitment Therapy while working through these processes:

## Wake up

This is all about cultivating a particular kind of awareness of your immediate present moment experience. To 'wake up' is to be present in the 'here and now', noticing the psychological traps and 'stories' that our minds tell us, which often hold us back in life. It refers to the ability to observe and watch your psychological experiences (in the form of thoughts, emotions, physical sensations) as they come and go, rather than being defined or controlled by them, when doing so is helpful. Practising *mindfulness* (of our internal and external world) is central to cultivating this present moment awareness. Mindfulness gives us a wider and higher perspective on our psychological experiences: as if we are the sky, and our thoughts and feelings are represented by the weather conditions passing through. Mindfulness is a key component of ACT, helping us to cultivate a greater awareness of our habitual, and sometimes unhelpful, responses to difficult psychological experiences.

## Loosen up

This is all about actively and purposely responding to your thoughts, emotions and physical sensations in a more open and accepting way, without judgement and defence. Rather than struggling with unwanted thoughts and feelings and trying to somehow change them, you can practise specific techniques that enable you to notice, stand back and loosen up around them, allowing them simply to be there as they naturally come and go. The result is a *willing and accepting stance* towards even your least desirable experiences, which can allow you to devote more time and energy to creating and living the life that really matters to you.

## Step up

This is all about identifying and clarifying what really brings meaning and fulfilment into your life – what it is that you really value and want your life to be about. With this clarification, you can set the chosen direction that you'd prefer your life to take and start to make some behavioural changes. You can choose to act in line with what you really want your life to be about, who you really want to be, and what you want to stand for in life. You can do this conscientiously, by setting and committing to specific goals and actions based on these qualities, more frequently over time, assured with the knowledge that even if these changes seem difficult or scary to make, they WILL be moving you towards living a life that is ultimately more rewarding and fulfilling. By 'stepping up' we choose to listen to our hearts and move with our feet, rather than always allowing our minds to direct our behaviour – particularly when doing so seems unhelpful.

Although for now we have introduced these three processes in a consecutive fashion, they all work simultaneously and interact with one another to foster greater psychological flexibility. We will, of course, be returning to all of this in a lot more detail in the chapters that follow. In the next chapters you will see how keeping these three processes alive – working side by side, moment by moment – is what ACT is really all about. The three terms *wake up*, *loosen up* and *step up* are not ACT terms per se, but we choose to use them as we think they encapsulate the essence of ACT.

Acceptance and Commitment Therapy really can offer you a new and sometimes more helpful perspective on the problems that you may be experiencing in life, as well as some alternative and really practical tools to help you get unstuck and move forwards – and we're really keen to show you how. So, whenever you are ready, do please read on ...

# 2 A radically different approach

In this chapter we will be returning to take a closer look at the psychological traps that we tend to get ourselves stuck in as human beings and also at how we can start to find our way out of these common pitfalls. This will hopefully lay a solid foundation and rationale for your further efforts in beginning to *wake up*, *loosen up* and *step up*, guided by the chapters that follow.

As we acknowledged in the previous chapter, like many people reading this book, you may have some aspects of yourself that you want to change. Perhaps you experience certain unwanted thoughts about yourself, other people, the future or the past. Maybe your mind is often full of worries and predictions about the worst that could happen, self-critical or self-doubting thoughts. You might experience seemingly overwhelming emotions, such as anxiety, anger, fear or sadness, to name just a few. Perhaps you're hoping that reading this book will help you to 'fix' these problems, in the same way a mechanic would fix a broken-down car or a painkiller might fix a headache.

This would be entirely understandable, particularly since this approach works very well when we consider physical health problems.

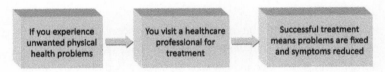

| If you experience unwanted physical health problems | You visit a healthcare professional for treatment | Successful treatment means problems are fixed and symptoms reduced |

Therefore, surely effective psychological treatments should have a similar objective, no? Success should be defined by the *reduction of unwanted psychological symptoms*?

This idea reflects most people's expectations about what books like this (and healthcare provision more generally) should be aiming to achieve. 'Feel less anxious!' 'Feel more confident!' 'Be more positive!' 'Get rid of your doubts and worries!' Surely, if we can get rid of unwanted thoughts and emotions and get more of the good, positive feelings, we should all feel much better.

Before exploring this idea in further detail, let's first identify the kinds of feelings and thoughts that you'd like to get rid of. These can sometimes be quite difficult to identify, so take your time to do this using the exercise below. We've listed some questions, that we hope might help you out. You might like to jot your answers down on a piece of paper or your mobile phone, tablet or laptop.

## Exercise 2.1

### What unwanted experiences do I try to eradicate?

What are the **emotions** that trouble you the most and you'd most like to reduce or get rid of? Try to identify an **emotion**, rather than a thought or a physical feeling. For example, anger, anxiety, sadness or jealousy.

The emotions I'd like to get rid of are ...

1. .............................................................................................

2. ......................................................................................

3. ......................................................................................

What are some of the **thoughts** that tend to cause you upset and you'd like to reduce or get rid of? Try to identify a **thought** here, rather than an emotion. Thoughts usually come in a collection of words that pop into our minds, but might also be images or memories. For example, '*Something bad is going to happen*', '*I'm not good enough*', '*I shouldn't have said/done that*', '*I'm a failure*', etc. These thoughts might be about yourself, other people, the future or the past, or a different situation entirely.

The thoughts I'd like to get rid of are ...

1. ......................................................................................

2. ...........................................................................................

3. ...........................................................................................

What are some of the **physical sensations** that feel
uncomfortable and you'd most like to reduce or get rid of?
For example, an increased heart rate, hot flushes, physical
shakes, persistent fatigue or aches and pains, discomfort in
your stomach, etc.?

The **physical sensations** I'd like to get rid of are ...

1. ...........................................................................................

2. ...........................................................................................

3. ...........................................................................................

## Quick-fix culture

Once you have completed the exercise above, let's return to the idea that if we can get rid of these unwanted emotions, thoughts and physical sensations in the same way that a medical doctor would help us get rid of a physical health problem, we should feel better, right?

We have all become accustomed to the idea that if we don't like an aspect of our lives, we can usually fix it. If we've got a headache, paracetamol can usually fix it. If we don't enjoy our jobs, we can try to fix it by seeking alternative employment. If we don't like an aspect of our physical appearance, we can usually fix it by changing our lifestyle, going shopping, having a haircut or even visiting a plastic surgeon! This 'fix it' rule has become so pervasive in modern lives that when we encounter unpleasant thoughts and feelings, we usually try to 'fix' these as well.

We imagine that you will already have tried a variety of different strategies in order to 'fix' the problems you've been experiencing and to reduce the psychological distress you're suffering.

We all do this, no matter whether our problems are debilitating enough to seek out professional support or whether we're talking about the everyday psychological challenges that we all experience (bad moods, self-doubt, critical thoughts about ourselves, worries, fears). Regardless of the severity of your difficulties, we're willing to bet you've tried various different things in order to help yourself feel better and to avoid or get rid of unpleasant emotions, thoughts and physical sensations. You may well have invested a huge amount of time, effort and resources into trying to help yourself feel better; it may even be the case that it is impossible to imagine trying harder than you have already. Your experience of doing so is what we ask you now to tap into.

In the exercise below, we would like you to make a list of the different things you've tried in the effort to fix the problems you've been experiencing. It might be helpful to jot this list down somewhere. We ask you to consider *anything* you have ever tried to do to avoid or get rid of unpleasant emotions, thoughts and physical sensations. In the box below we've listed some of the things people might do, but your list might be entirely different. Consider not only the ways you've tried to change how you're feeling, but also the ways in which you might have changed your life. Maybe you've found yourself starting or stopping certain activities. Maybe you've started avoiding certain people, places or situations. Maybe you've tried to implement various different thinking tools you've heard about before. Perhaps you've been taking prescribed medications (or other non-licensed substances) to fix your problems.

**Exercise 2.2**

The strategies I have used to avoid, get rid of or 'fix' unpleasant emotions, thoughts or physical sensations

**Avoidance:** Have you ever avoided or withdrawn from people, places, activities, situations or events because you felt bad or wanted to avoid feeling bad? For example, avoiding job interviews or work meetings, avoiding large groups of people, avoiding parties, avoiding being alone, avoiding dates, or staying in bed?

**Taking your mind off it:** How have you tried to distract yourself or keep your mind off unwanted emotions, thoughts or physical sensations? For example, watching TV, working non-stop, exercising excessively, playing computer games, using your mobile phone, listening to loud music.

**Things you've used to try to feel better:** For example, using food, alcohol, medication, drugs, gambling, sex, self-harm, researching your condition online, getting reassurance from doctors.

**Thinking strategies:** How have you tried to think your way to feeling better when unwanted emotions, thoughts or physical sensations show up? For example, rationalising, worrying, thinking about the past, fantasising about the future, analysing yourself or your situation, imagining certain escape scenarios, day dreaming, thinking positively, thinking negatively, criticising yourself or blaming others, blocking certain thoughts.

**Doing more of certain things:** For example, exercise, relaxation, yoga, deep breathing, positive self-talk, complimentary medicines, psychological therapy.

**Anything else at all you have tried?**

## Have these strategies worked for you?

Once you've given these questions some thought, we would like you to consider how well each of these strategies has worked for you by completing Exercise 2.3. There is no right or wrong answer to this; we simply ask you to tune in to your own experience. For each of the strategies you have listed above, we ask you to consider:

- Did this strategy help you to feel better in the shorter term?

- Did this strategy help you to feel better in the longer term?

- Were there any other effects or consequences of using this strategy upon your quality of life?

## Exercise 2.3

### How well have these strategies been working?

We've completed a few examples in the table below based on what other people we've met have shared with us, and then created a blank table where you might consider your own experience.

| What have you tried? | Did it make you feel better? | | Were there any other effects on your quality of life? |
|---|---|---|---|
| | In the shorter term? | In the longer term? | |
| Trying to think positively | Yes | No – it was hard to maintain and frustrating | None |

| Drinking a lot of alcohol | Yes – it helped to block things out | No – I felt worse | I started doing things I regretted, it's not good for my health and I wasted lots of money |
| Worrying a lot | No, I felt worse | No – I felt stuck | I couldn't concentrate and my partner got frustrated with me |
| Yoga | Yes, I felt better | Yes, I felt better | Improved my fitness and I made a new friend |
| Keeping very busy at work | Yes – it kept my mind occupied | No – I felt exhausted | I was too tired to spend time with friends |

| Making lists | Yes – it helped me to feel more in control | No, I felt overwhelmed – I never made it through the lists | I never seemed to get anything done, so I stopped wanting to do anything! |

We suggest copying out the following template onto a piece of paper (or an electronic device) and then using it to consider how the strategies you identified in Exercise 2.2 have been working for you.

| What have you tried? | Did it make you feel better? | | Were there any other effects on your quality of life? |
|---|---|---|---|
| | In the shorter term? | In the longer term? | |
| 1<br>2<br>3. etc. | | | |

## What does your *experience* tell you?

If you've been following the 'fix it' rule and trying to use a range of different strategies designed to avoid, reduce or get rid of unwanted emotions, thoughts and physical sensations, your table is probably looking rather full. It's important to emphasise that we don't mean to suggest there is anything inherently 'wrong' with these strategies. They are entirely normal and most people would have tried to help themselves in exactly the same way. Remember, the 'fix it' rule is pervasive! We simply encourage you to spend a few moments thinking about whether these strategies have really been working for you, particularly in the longer term, and whether there has been any unwanted impact upon your quality of life.

As you reflect on your experience of using these strategies, what do you notice? How well have they been working? Are your problems better, worse or about the same than they were three months ago? Have there been any costs of these strategies in terms of your quality of life? What about your energy reserves, time, money, work, relationships?

If the things you've been doing to avoid, control, reduce or get rid of your unwanted thoughts and feelings have been working, and have had no unwanted consequences upon your quality of life, then there's no problem. We don't want to interfere with anything that seems to be working for you, so do please carry on!

As we discussed briefly in the previous chapter, sometimes these 'fix it' strategies don't work so well. They might bring some short-term relief, but don't necessarily help us feel better in the longer term. In fact they may even make us feel worse. What's more, these strategies can often have unwanted consequences upon our wider quality of life. Avoiding places where we feel anxious can lead to life becoming restricted. Worrying a lot about the future can reduce our ability to concentrate and focus on the 'here and now'. Keeping busy to avoid feeling anxious can leave us feeling exhausted. Staying in bed to avoid facing the world can leave us feeling even more fed up and isolated by the end of the day. Avoiding a job interview can restrict our career opportunities and further reduce our confidence. Avoiding close and loving relationships to protect ourselves from the pain of loss or a relationship breakdown can mean we miss out on the joy of intimacy, love and having someone to care for (and care for us). To explore this point in a slightly different way, please have a go at the next exercise, Exercise 2.4.

## Exercise 2.4
### Push away your 'pain'

The strategies we use to control, reduce, avoid or eliminate unwanted emotions, thoughts and physical sensations can sometimes leave us feeling stuck and take us away from doing things that matter to us. They can also bring even more suffering into our lives. Let's take a moment or two to explore this in a slightly different way, with the following exercise:

If you're reading indoors, then please either stand up or ensure that from where you are sitting you can place your hand firmly against a wall (if you're outside you can improvise by planting your feet firmly on the ground). Imagine that everything you want to avoid or get rid of is contained within that wall (or the ground). Now, (as you would normally try to get rid of unwanted experiences) try pushing against the wall with your hand (or the ground with your feet). And, as you keep doing this, notice what happens.

No doubt your body is starting to feel pretty strained. If you did that for any length of time you'd probably start to feel achy and tired. Along with this physical tension and tiredness (which tends to result from pushing away thoughts and emotions), consider also if you were pushing against the wall/ground all day long. How well could you engage in doing things that matter to you?

Keep pushing against the wall/ground and consider how well you could help a friend, succeed at work, contribute to the community, take care of yourself; how well could you physically type at a keyboard, give someone you cherish a hug or do something caring for someone important?

When you're ready, please stop pushing against the wall/ ground and notice the release of tension as you do so ...

What do you make of that?

## Sinking in quicksand

To put this idea another way, sometimes trying to control, reduce, avoid or eliminate unwanted thoughts and emotions (however we do it!) can be a bit like getting caught in quicksand. If you were stuck in quicksand, your natural instinct would be to try to escape, yet everything you've learned about how to escape would lead you to sink even deeper. Your instinct is to struggle, yet your experience tells you that the more you struggle, the deeper you seem to sink.

If you found a friend who was caught in quicksand and you could see that every time they struggled they sunk that little bit further, what would be the first thing you'd want them to do? In all likelihood, the very first thing you'd ask them to do would be to stop! Stop struggling! This would probably be a rather disconcerting message for your friend to hear, particularly since every part of them will want to continue struggling to try to help themselves get free. What's more, your friend's mind will continue to encourage them to struggle because it can't see any other options. Yet your message will be to do the total opposite – stop struggling, get into full contact with the quicksand, maximise surface area and stay still.

Of course, this doesn't mean that your friend instantly becomes free and liberated, but at least the situation won't be getting any worse, and other ways of *responding* to the quicksand might become available.

A similar approach can also sometimes be helpful when it comes to responding to unwanted thoughts and feelings. When your experience of doing things to avoid or get rid of these thoughts and feelings tells you that these strategies are not working for you, and perhaps are pulling you even deeper into the quicksand, then a radically different approach is required.

## Stop the struggle and set yourself free

ACT (and therefore this book) offers a radically different approach. As you read on, you'll discover a range of skills and techniques designed to help you *manage difficult thoughts and feelings more effectively*, when it seems helpful to do so, so you can devote more time and energy to *doing the things that matter* to you in life.

The implications of this are really important to consider, so let's pause to think about it carefully.

Our aim is to **manage difficult thoughts and feelings more effectively** ... what exactly are we saying here?

What we're *not* saying is that this book can help you avoid, reduce or get rid of these thoughts and feelings. In some respects, this might come as quite a shock. Many people assume that psychologists should aim to help people feel better through helping them to learn to control, reduce or eliminate the unwanted thoughts and feelings they've been experiencing.

However, perhaps in other respects this idea is not so shocking. If we told you that this brief book can help you to get rid of unwanted thoughts and emotions, would you really have believed us? 'Feel less anxious! Feel more confident! Be more positive! Get rid of your doubts and worries!' Would you believe us if we claimed we could help you be rid of these painful (yet entirely normal and human) psychological experiences? What's more, we discussed earlier in this chapter how trying to control, avoid or eliminate these experiences can sometimes lead to further difficulties. Are human emotions and thoughts *really* problems to be solved, controlled, reduced or eliminated? The definition of a problem is something that has a solution. Do emotions have solutions? Or are thoughts and emotions (positive and negative) an inescapable part of being human? Maybe, just maybe, you might consider 'taking them along with you for the ride' knowing that if you're willing to do so, you get to be more like the person you truly want to be and to live a life more like the one you truly want to have.

So, although 'hitting the feel-good button' and seeking to eliminate our painful experiences might initially seem like the best option, there are often costs associated with doing so; life can shrink and we can become more distant from what we really care about. In fact, when you really think about it, 'hitting the feel-good button and keeping it firmly pressed down' in life can ultimately lead to feeling nothing at all – life can start to feel pretty empty and meaningless. But where does that leave you?

Clearly, something still has to change. The assumption we started with at the beginning of this chapter was that there was something in your life you wanted to change. So, what *could* you do? Where should this 'radically different approach' begin? Where should you start? Where should you focus your energy? Well, let's take a look at that right now.

## What will you do if nothing you do will do?

Throughout this chapter we've been looking at whether the strategies you've been using to help yourself have been working effectively. There have been no right or wrong answers, instead we've been encouraging you to take a pragmatic stance by asking yourself whether these strategies have been working effectively in terms of moving you forward towards the kind of life you want to have.

Let's continue with this pragmatic approach by considering where you *can* achieve change. What can you control? Surely your efforts should be best directed towards the parts of your life in which you can exert influence. Let's look at where this might be possible.

We'll think about each of these, one at a time.

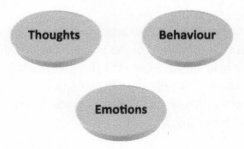

## Can we control our thoughts?

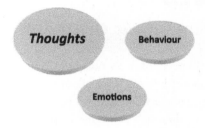

'Don't worry about it!' 'Try not to give it too much thought.' 'You need to think positively.' 'Just try and distract yourself!'

We are all used to receiving messages from people around us telling us that we should be able to control our thoughts. Putting aside this common wisdom for a second, what's your experience of actually trying to do this? How easy is it to stop worrying or to banish certain thoughts from your mind? Please take a few moments to reflect on your experience of actually trying to do this.

Let's explore this with an exercise.

## Exercise 2.5 🚲
### Don't think about chocolate!

For the next 30 seconds, we would like you to avoid thinking about chocolate. Try not to think about how chocolate might taste, smell or appear. Push all thoughts about chocolate entirely out of your mind. Think about absolutely anything you want, try to distract your mind and push away any thoughts about chocolate ... Start the timer ... Go!

So how did that go? Your experience of trying to avoid thinking about chocolate was probably characterised by a well-known finding in psychology called 'the re-bound effect'. This refers to the experience of trying to push thoughts away, and inevitably thinking the very thought you're trying to avoid! Much like throwing a tennis ball against a brick wall – the more effort you put into throwing the thought away, the more powerfully it bounces back towards you.

Even if you managed to take your mind off chocolate – where did your mind go instead? Wherever it went, whatever you thought about – how did you know you were being successful? Probably because whatever you were thinking about was not chocolate – and sure enough, inevitably you're back thinking about CHOCOLATE again!

This re-bound effect often occurs when people experience frightening, threatening, unusual or unwanted thoughts. These thoughts are unpleasant to experience and understandably people employ the 'fix it' rule and respond by trying to push these thoughts away or block them out. Unfortunately, this response often exacerbates the frequency and impact of these unwanted thoughts, as you may have just experienced in the above exercise.

So, the problem here is not necessarily the thought itself, but rather the way in which we *respond* to that thought. Therefore, perhaps we have much less control over the thoughts we experience than we often give ourselves credit for. On this basis, maybe it's best to allow your thoughts to be as they are (more on how to do this in the 'Loosen up!' chapter), and perhaps our efforts to exert control should be directed elsewhere.

## Can we control our emotions?

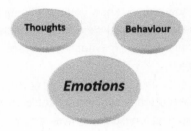

'Cheer up!' 'Calm down!' 'Just relax.' 'There's no need to get angry!'

We all receive these messages from the world and people around us, suggesting that we should be able to control our emotions. Once again, putting aside this common wisdom for a second, what's your experience of actually trying to do this?

Have you ever woken up one day and for some reason felt grumpy? How easy has it been to make yourself feel differently? You may have continued with the day and noticed that with time your emotions change, but, in that grumpy moment, how easy was it to change how you felt?

What about before an examination, a performance or another important event – how easy has it been to stop feeling anxious, no matter how many times you told yourself to calm down? What about when you've noticed feelings such as anger, sadness, distress, humiliation or embarrassment – how easy has it been to stop feeling these feelings?

Sometimes we are able to avoid feeling certain feelings. Strategies such as drinking alcohol, using drugs, being very busy or keeping your mind occupied can all help to keep unwanted emotions at bay. Unfortunately, these 'fix it' strategies may not last very long and often have unwanted consequences. What's more, keeping emotions at bay in this way can sometimes be like trying to hold a tightly blown-up beach ball underneath the water in a swimming pool. It takes effort, concentration and quickly becomes tiring. What's more, when our attention becomes distracted or something else happens, the beach ball can rush to the surface with an enormous splash in a way that seems unpredictable, overwhelming and very difficult to deal with.

If your experience is anything like ours, we reach an inescapable conclusion: our emotions are often nowhere near as easy to control as we all like to think. Let's explore this by considering 'The polygraph machine' scenario on the following page.

## The polygraph machine
### (Hayes, Strosahl & Wilson, 2003)

Imagine we take a group of volunteers into a laboratory. We attach each person's right arm to a polygraph machine. Polygraph machines (or 'lie-detectors') work by monitoring an individual's level of physiological arousal, which is closely associated with anxiety. Imagine that we instruct all volunteers to avoid feeling anxious. To raise the stakes a little, we attach each person's index finger to a safe but painful electric shock machine. We emphasise that nobody will receive an electric shock unless the polygraph machine detects physiological signs of anxiety. If the polygraph machine detects any signs of anxiety, a small but painful electric shock will automatically be delivered. What do you imagine might happen?

Surely, some level of anxiety (and therefore an electric shock!) would be inevitable for most people! Of course, it's unlikely that any of us will ever be attached to a polygraph machine next time we feel anxious. However, we all possess a system capable of much greater sensitivity than even the world's very best polygraph machine – our central nervous system! Our central nervous system responds to even the slightest change in physiological arousal.

So, what chance does any of us have at being able to not feel anxious within situations we experience as anxiety-provoking? What chance do any of us have of avoiding feeling anger when we are angry? What chance do any of us have at not feeling emotions when we are *feeling* emotional?

Instead, perhaps you can relate to the following approach to emotion: if you're not willing to have it, you've got it! Perhaps the key to experiencing unwanted emotions as manageable rather than overwhelming is, ironically, to allow ourselves to feel those emotions – more on this in Chapter 4.

Similarly, can we control the frequency and intensity of the positive emotions we experience? If we asked you to feel a great sense of happiness right now, could you do it? If we asked you to go outside right now and fall in love, could you do it?

So, perhaps we have much less control over the emotions we experience than we give ourselves credit for.

## Can we control our behaviour?

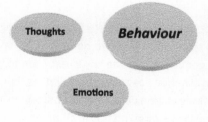

What about behaviour? Can you control what you do right now? Regardless of the thoughts, emotions or physical sensations you are experiencing right now, can you exert control over what you do in the next few seconds?

Our behaviour is clearly the area in which we have greatest control. Our ability to choose what we do is far, far greater than our ability to choose what we think and feel.

Indeed, is it possible to *feel* a certain way yet choose to *behave* differently? Have you ever felt afraid and behaved courageously? Have you ever felt tired and behaved energetically? Have you ever felt disappointed with a gift and responded in a polite and gracious manner?

Similarly, is it possible to *think* in a certain way, yet choose to *behave* differently? Have you ever thought you can't go on, and yet continued? Please have a go at the following exercise to explore whether we can behave in a certain way, even when our mind might tell us otherwise ...

## Exercise 2.6
### *Raise your right arm*

Could you have the thought '*I can't raise my right arm*' and raise your right arm anyway? What do you reckon? Well, let's try it right now.

Just for the next few moments, we ask you to really focus and concentrate as hard as you can on the thought '*I can't raise my right arm*'. Start now and keep repeating this thought, silently if you like in your mind, and really buy into it. '*I can't raise my right arm. I can't raise my right arm.*'

Now, while you continue to concentrate on thinking that thought, please raise your right arm.

What does that simple exercise tell us about the relationship between our thoughts and behaviour? Well, although we all become very used to listening to the thoughts we experience and using them to guide our actions, this doesn't always have to be the case. In fact, our minds may tell us all sorts of things that are not always helpful to be listening to!

## Where does this leave you?

By now you may well be wondering how all these ideas can help. This is entirely normal, completely understandable and, actually, a very good place to start. You may also be feeling rather confused and wondering how on earth all of this is going to help you move forward. What should you *do* next?

Well, that's a difficult question to answer. Whatever you do next, it might be something that's different from what you've done before – particularly if what you've done before hasn't been working. Remember, when we say 'working' we encourage you to consider whether what you are doing is moving you towards being the kind of person you want to be and living the sort of life you would prefer to have, or not. Whatever you do next could be orientated around this question, rather than focused on controlling, avoiding, reducing or eliminating the unwanted thoughts and feelings you've been experiencing. You are the best person to choose what to do next. What this book can offer you is a range of strategies, exercises and techniques that can sometimes help people to move forward towards the kind of life they want while taking any unwanted thoughts and feelings with them. Therefore, the stance you may choose to adopt from this point onwards could be:

*I'm having these really difficult thoughts, sensations and emotions,*

*AND*

*I'm willing to take them with me as I move towards the things that matter to me in life.*

Considering everything we've discussed so far, that might be starting to sound like a more helpful approach. Yet you may still be noticing a little apprehension, which is entirely normal and absolutely fine. As this point, we would like to introduce another metaphor. This is actually a metaphor that we will be revisiting, exploring and elaborating in the chapters that follow, as we take a closer look at how we can *wake up, loosen up* and *step up*. So, take a look at the following scenario, consider it for a moment or two, and then see where it leaves you.

## The path forwards

Imagine that you're cycling along a track one day and you reach a fork in the path. One way is the route you've taken on many occasions in the past and is a well-worn track. It's reasonably clear, with no significant obstacles, and you know where it takes you. If you were cycling on autopilot, you would automatically turn down this path without hesitation. The second track is overgrown, thick with brambles and full of potholes. You've never taken this path before and it looks like a difficult, menacing and arduous route. Which path would you choose?

Now, what if we told you that everything that's important to you, everything that you care about deeply in your life lies along that second path? Now, which path would you choose?

Still feeling uneasy or unsure? Well, that's absolutely fine. When we do new things, and especially when those things are important to us, it's entirely normal to feel apprehensive or uncertain. Before we move on to take a look at exactly how ACT can help us, let's recap some of the main ideas and learning points from this chapter.

## Chapter 2 summary points

- Sometimes our experience of trying to control, avoid, fix or get rid of unwanted thoughts and emotions can be a bit like struggling in quicksand. The more we try to control or avoid unwanted thoughts and emotions, the deeper we end up sinking. We find ourselves stuck and unable to move forward.

- In this way, the problem isn't so much the presence of unwanted thoughts or feelings, but the way we *respond* to them or try to exert control over these psychological experiences.

- If we do want to make some changes in life, the best place to start is where we have most control - our behaviour.

- There is an alternative to trying to control, reduce, avoid or get rid of our unwanted thoughts and feelings, which can sometimes be a more helpful approach. There's much more on this in the chapters that follow.

# 3 Wake up!

So, you've decided to continue on your journey through this book, at least for now, which is great news! We hope that, as you continue reading and experimenting with the exercises, you might start to share our appreciation of how ACT can help us all to live a richer, fuller and more meaningful life. In this chapter we will take a closer look at some of the main ideas and skills that ACT offers and, in particular, how it can help us to **wake up**. What do we actually mean by 'wake up'? Well, let's put this into some context straight away by expanding on the metaphor that we ended Chapter 2 with.

## The path forwards

Imagine that you're cycling along a track one day and you reach a fork in the path. One way is the route you've taken on many occasions in the past and is a well-worn track. It's reasonably clear, with no significant obstacles, and you know where it takes you. If you were cycling on autopilot, you would automatically turn down this path without hesitation. The second track is overgrown, thick with brambles and full of potholes. You've never taken this path before, and it looks like a difficult, menacing and arduous route. Which path would you choose?

Now, what if we told you that everything that's important to you, everything that you care about deeply in your life, lies along that second path? Now, which path would you choose?

If your chosen route were the second path, what would actually be involved in making that choice? Well, first of all, you'd need to *notice* (and wake up to) your autopilot tendency to take the first path. You'd also need to *notice* (and wake up to) the option to take the second path, with everything that comes with it. Only then, with this kind of *noticing* and *awareness*, could you *choose* what to do ...

## Turning off the autopilot

*'If we don't decide where we're going, we're bound to end up where we're headed.'*

*— Hayes, Strosahl & Wilson, 2003*

'Autopilot' usually refers to an electronic system that controls a vehicle's direction of travel, without much 'hands on' or conscious control by a human pilot or driver. This can often be a very effective means of travelling, which gives the pilot or driver a break from the effort involved in controlling the vehicle. However, sometimes being on autopilot can become a less effective means of travel, particularly if we wish to move in a different direction along a less familiar route. In this case, a more conscious, flexible and 'hands-on' approach may be required.

In much the same way, many of us spend a lot of time on a kind of 'psychological autopilot'. We become used to being driven through life by the thoughts or emotions that our minds create. This can often work well, and allows us to navigate our way through life without always needing to be alert or aware, or consciously making decisions. For example, you may have got out of bed, showered and dressed this morning in a way that didn't require much awareness or conscious decision-making. In this respect, your mind was in charge of your behaviour and didn't need too much supervision. Indeed, when we're on autopilot our thoughts and emotions drive us through life without much hands-on and conscious control. In many ways this can be an efficient and helpful way of navigating our way through life.

Sometimes, however, this 'psychological autopilot' can become less helpful. Being automatically driven through life by our thoughts or emotions can drive us away from what we truly want to do. For example, responding on autopilot to thoughts such as *she's not being fair* can lead us to behave in a less caring manner than we might choose towards a loved one. Responding on autopilot to fear or anxiety can lead us to leave or avoid places or situations we might otherwise choose to remain in. Responding on autopilot to negative, critical or unhelpful thoughts about ourselves might lead us to take these thoughts seriously, as if our mind always produces thoughts that are 100% accurate and should be followed, believed or acted upon!

Therefore, when this 'psychological autopilot' is not driving us in a helpful direction, perhaps a different approach is warranted. In this chapter we'll look at what this different approach might involve. We'll explore what might be involved in helping ourselves to wake up and switch off the autopilot when it seems helpful to do so.

Before going any further however, it might be useful to look at the kinds of thoughts we usually listen to when we're on autopilot and the way our minds usually work. Let's look at the thoughts our minds produce with the following exercise.

## Exercise 3.1 🚲
*Watching your thoughts*

This exercise is not about changing anything, but simply about noticing the thoughts your mind produces in a given moment. In a few seconds we'll ask you to close your eyes and follow the instructions below. We suggest you read through the instructions a few times before getting going, so you don't have to remind yourself about what to do during the exercise.

- Find a comfortable place to sit. This isn't a relaxation exercise, so try to maintain a relatively alert posture.

- When you're ready, and once you've read through the instructions, please close your eyes.

- Focus your attention on the sensations involved in breathing in and out. Simply bring your attention to noticing how the air feels a bit cooler as you breathe in and a bit warmer as you breathe out. Simply notice these temperature sensations, along with other sensations in your chest and abdomen as your diaphragm and muscles help you to breathe that breath.

■ Try for a while to only focus on your breath, including the sensations and rhythm of your breathing – just tracking one breath at a time – the best you can.

■ During this exercise, your mind will almost certainly wander away from your breath – this is entirely normal and to be expected. It's common for our minds to be distracted by thoughts. Every time your mind wanders, simply *notice* the thought that is entering into your mind. Don't try to change it in any way or push it away; there's also no need to get caught up in the thought either – simply acknowledge it. Then, gently escort your attention back to focusing on your breath.

■ Carry on this exercise until you've given yourself sufficient opportunity to *notice* the kinds of thoughts that show up; about three minutes should be enough, but the exact time isn't important.

## What kinds of thoughts do our minds usually produce?

So what did you notice? You probably found that your mind was producing all kinds of thoughts. Thoughts about what you were hearing or feeling. Perhaps thoughts about what you're doing later, or something that happened earlier. Maybe you noticed thoughts about when to bring the exercise itself to an end; or about whether you might be doing the exercise correctly or incorrrectly. Maybe you noticed thoughts about the exercise seeming helpful or unhelpful, useful or pointless, easy or difficult; or maybe you even had thoughts about the thoughts you were noticing!

Whatever you noticed, you probably found that your mind was rather busy. Some of your thoughts may have been about what you were doing *right now* and maybe they were evaluating or judging your experience in some way. However, many of your thoughts were perhaps about something in the future or the past.

## Our minds tend to time travel

Our ability to think about the past or the future appears to be one of the most useful abilities of our mind. It allows us to learn from our experience, to plan for the future and to navigate our way through life in a way that seems to be incredibly helpful. If you consider almost every aspect of human endeavour, our achievements owe much to our mind's ability to 'time travel' in this way.

Clearly, our ability to think about the past or the future can help us to solve many of the problems we encounter in everyday life. If you've made a mistake, you may want to think about what happened so you can do things differently next time. If you've got an important event coming up, you'll need to plan for the future in an effort to be well prepared.

However, sometimes this ability to zoom into the past or future can become less helpful. When we are going through a difficult time in life, or feeling anxious, depressed or another form of distress, our minds rarely wander to happy places. Indeed, this tendency of our minds to travel backwards or forwards in time is so common when people are suffering that psychologists have terms for it. 'Rumination' refers to the process of thinking repetitively about something that has happened in the past, while 'worry' refers to the process of rehearsing something that might happen in the future. When our minds do this, we often end up feeling worse. What can also happen is that our minds travel to some kind of fantasy or desired outcome in the future, which, although seemingly pleasant, can make returning to the present moment seem even worse.

Most importantly, however, when our minds are time-travelling into the past or the future, we aren't fully focused on opportunities available in the 'here and now'. We're not focusing on the present, which can reduce our ability to engage fully with our lives as they are actually happening. We can miss out on meaningful and fulfilling experiences. Take a look at John's situation to see what we mean.

John had been out of work for a couple of months and was beginning to worry about ever finding another job. Every time he attended a job interview he became highly anxious. The night before his next interview, John found himself lying in bed, kept awake by thoughts of every single job interview he'd 'failed' at in the past. His mind also provided him with a number of pessimistic predictions about the future – *'You'll screw it up'*, *'They'll think you're hopeless'*, *'They won't be interested in you'*. The next morning, after a night of very little sleep, John woke up feeling exhausted, and so decided to make a phone call to cancel his job interview arranged for later that day.

That evening, his wife suggested they go out for dinner to try to take John's mind off things. Throughout dinner, John was preoccupied by regrets about cancelling his interview earlier that day, and also by worries about how he'd never be able to progress in his career. He snapped at his wife when she tried to talk about other things and this led to an argument during which John's wife complained that he seemed constantly distracted and never able to spend any quality time with her any more. Meanwhile, John continued to feel preoccupied by thoughts about what might have been and worried about the future and, as a consequence, completely missed out on the evening with his wife.

Maybe you can relate to John's situation at times? Perhaps you find that you too can become so caught up with thoughts about the future or the past (or both) that you start to feel worse and/ or miss out on what is actually happening in the here and now? Take a moment or two to have a go at the following exercise to see where your own mind tends to travel to.

## Exercise 3.2 🚲
### Your time-travelling mind

Have a think about your time-travelling mind before you read on. Where does your mind most commonly time-travel to?

- Maybe in a meeting at work you find yourself thinking about what you just said a few minutes ago or about what you need to do later.

- Perhaps while trying to concentrate on a piece of work or a television programme (or even this book!) you are thinking about what you'll be doing later on or having for dinner.

■ Maybe while you are chatting with your friend/partner, you find yourself thinking about what you want to do or say next rather than listening to them.

Whether or not any of these scenarios sounds familiar to you, can you also identify any costs or unwanted consequences of focusing on thoughts about the past or the future, rather than focusing your awareness on the present moment, which you are actually living in?

Many of the thoughts we usually experience on autopilot mode are about the past or the future. Particularly when we already feel anxious or depressed, the tendency of our minds to time-travel can sometimes be unhelpful.

At the start of this chapter we set out to explore what might be involved in helping ourselves to wake up and switch off the autopilot when it's helpful to do so. A key aspect of doing so is often to notice when our minds are time-travelling and, instead, to *deliberately bring our awareness into the present moment*. We'll be returning to this point and how to practise doing this very soon. Before we do so, how else do our minds usually work?

## Our minds are judgemental

During Exercise 3.1 you may have noticed thoughts about the exercise seeming helpful or unhelpful, useful or pointless, easy or difficult. This is another way in which our minds usually work; our minds excel at judging or evaluating various aspects of ourselves, our experience, others and the world.

As we saw in the previous chapter, when our minds judge a particular thought or emotion as unwanted, unpleasant or somehow negative, we often automatically slip into the 'fix it' mode and do things to try to get rid of that unwanted thought or feeling – for example, distraction, avoidance, escape, or attempts to control. As we discussed, this 'fix it' approach can often result in life becoming narrower and lead us to behave in a manner we might not choose to.

Another key aspect of switching off the autopilot mode is therefore to take a *non-judgemental and curious attitude* towards each aspect of our current experience – including thoughts and emotions (the exercises that follow will help you to practise this too).

## Our minds tend to be rigid

When we're on autopilot mode we tend to become rather rigid. We become rigid in the way we think about things. We begin to relate to our thoughts as facts, truths or commands that must be followed and we then become rigid in the way we do things. We assume that the way we see things is the 'right' way to see them. We create rules for how we should behave, or how we expect others to. Once again, listening to our thoughts and responding accordingly can often be very helpful. However, when we feel low, anxious, angry or afraid, or experience difficult, critical, frightening or self-defeating thoughts, it can be less helpful to listen to our thoughts. Instead of using how we feel and what we think to guide our behaviour, we can learn to relate to our thoughts and emotions in a more flexible way when doing so seems helpful.

Sometimes it can be very helpful to focus on one aspect of our current experience. If we're at work or watching a film, we want our awareness to be focused and narrow. At other times it can be helpful to broaden our awareness to notice many different aspects of our current experience, including whatever we are currently doing, feeling, thinking, seeing, touching, hearing, smelling and tasting. Therefore, another key aspect of this skill is to be *flexible* (again you can practise this in just a moment).

In summary, being automatically driven through life by our thoughts or emotions can sometimes drive us away from what we truly want to do. When set on autopilot, our minds tend to travel backwards and forwards in time, judging aspects of our experience as wanted or unwanted, and tend to be very rigid. In order to 'wake up' we need to switch off the autopilot mode by using our awareness to *deliberately focus on the present moment, with a non-judgemental, curious and flexible attitude*. A skill that can help us to do this is **mindfulness**. For readers who are already familiar with mindfulness, you might recognise some of the exercises that follow and we hope you find them useful. For anyone who has not come across mindfulness before, we hope you will find this a good place to start!

**Tuning in to the present moment**

The way in which we can tune in to the present moment has its roots in mindfulness. Mindfulness is difficult to define, because it is both a state of mind and a set of skills. In essence, mindfulness means:

*Deliberately focusing on the present moment, with a non-judgemental, curious and flexible attitude.*

As with many of the new ideas presented in this book, it can be more helpful to practise an exercise rather than reading words on a page – just like when you learn to ride a bike – so let's go straight into a mindfulness exercise now.

**Exercise 3.3**
*Mindfulness of your body*

■ Wherever you are sitting or standing right now, take a moment to notice some of the physical sensations involved in sitting/standing. *Deliberately* and from a *curious* stance notice any sensations of touch and pressure where your body makes contact with the seat or where your feet make contact with the floor.

■ As best you can, continue to hold these physical sensations at centre stage in your awareness. Notice how perhaps they come and go, change in intensity or stay the same.

■ If your mind wanders away from these sensations, that is entirely normal. Each time your mind wanders, just notice this, congratulate yourself for noticing it and then deliberately and gently guide your awareness back to any one of these sensations in your body, again and again.

■ Please continue to practise this for a few minutes and whenever you feel ready you can end the exercise.

You can do this practice at anytime, anywhere, and you might prefer to do it for longer periods and/or with your eyes closed to limit further visual distractions.

How did you find that? Please take a few minutes to reflect on your experience of running through that exercise.

There are a number of common things people experience when they begin to use mindfulness. Let's discuss some of those common experiences here:

### It was really difficult!

That's a common experience. Tuning in to an aspect of the present moment can be difficult. In many ways, we are training our minds in much the same way as we train our muscles in the gym. With practice and repetition we will build new muscle fibres, which develop over time into bigger, stronger muscles. A similar process occurs when we start to train ourselves to tune in to the present moment.

### I couldn't keep my mind focused on what I was meant to be doing, it kept wandering off!

As we said, that's entirely normal and to be expected. It's not something you need to stop happening. Our minds have evolved to be constantly on the move, and in many circumstances this is extremely helpful. We certainly can't just 'turn this off' when we practise mindfulness.

How should we respond to this tendency of our minds to wander off? It's important to remember we are training our minds to use a new skill when we use mindfulness. Have you ever trained a puppy (or any other small being for that matter)? Imagine if a puppy dashed into the room right now, scampering this way and that, sniffing your shoes, chewing your bag, scratching this, pawing at that ...

How would that puppy respond if you tried to train him by shouting at and berating him for not following instructions, while yanking his collar and becoming frustrated and punishing him? Would that be an effective teaching strategy? Or would a gentler, patient, kind, persistent and rewarding approach be called for?

Punishment is not an effective strategy for shaping new behaviour. The second approach is probably the more effective learning strategy and is similar to the approach we need to take when we're using mindfulness. Wandering minds are entirely normal, and every time we notice our minds have wandered off we have another opportunity to congratulate ourselves for *noticing* what is happening in the present moment (because that's what mindfulness is!), and then gently, patiently and kindly guide our attention back to the task.

### I found it really relaxing

This is an entirely normal, pleasant and very understandable consequence of participating in a mindfulness exercise – particularly if you had your eyes closed! However, relaxation is not the goal of mindfulness. As we said, the aim is to wake up, not doze off! Indeed, mindfulness exercises require an active and alert approach (although feeling relaxed is a welcome and very common by-product).

## Mindfulness is not a control strategy

Now, you may be hoping that mindfulness will help you achieve your goal of being able to exert control or influence over the unwanted thoughts and feelings you experience. You might be hoping that mindfulness can help you clear your mind of stressful thoughts and get rid of all your unpleasant feelings.

This is not the goal of tuning in to the present moment. In fact, when we are being mindful we are not aiming to 'achieve' anything. Instead, the purpose is simply to cultivate your awareness of the present moment; to deliberately notice your thoughts, emotions and other aspects of your ongoing experience, as they naturally come and go, as they rise and fall, with an *open*, *accepting* and *curious* attitude.

Crucially, this gives us the opportunity to *choose* how to respond to these thoughts and feelings. This is a really key point. There are other ways of responding to unwanted thoughts and feelings, rather than falling back on strategies designed to control, avoid or fix unwanted thoughts and emotions, particularly when doing so leaves you feeling stuck (remember the quicksand metaphor in the previous chapter?) and leads to unwanted consequences.

Tuning in to the present moment involves bringing flexible and deliberate attention to your experience as it happens – to observe thoughts, feelings and physical sensations, rather than getting stuck to them. Present moment awareness is all about noticing these experiences, accepting them for what they are and allowing them to be.

To summarise this section, there are many benefits of mindfulness:

■ When we feel anxious, worried, angry or low in mood we often spend a lot of time psychologically travelling into the past or into the future. We find ourselves thinking over and over again about something that has already happened; alternatively, we become preoccupied by worries about things that haven't yet occurred. This is not always a helpful thing to do – particularly if it leaves us feeling worse and reduces our awareness and ability to respond effectively to the present moment. Mindfulness can help us to gently escort our attention back into the present moment, so we can then decide what we want to do. From awareness, comes choice!

■ Mindfulness can help us to sharpen our attention, so we are more fully focused on what we're doing.

■ Mindfulness can help us become more aware of our autopilot tendencies and what our minds are up to; it can help us to respond more effectively to unwanted thoughts and feelings.

■ By connecting fully with the present, we can experience ongoing events in a much richer way. Whether we're out with friends, exercising or simply enjoying a shower, deliberately paying attention to that experience rather than being lost in other thoughts or worries can really increase our ability to enjoy and connect with everything life has to offer.

Along with the exercises above, you might like to continue practising mindfulness in other ways. There really are so many opportunities to practise, and you don't have to be alone in a darkened room with your eyes closed. You can practise anywhere and with any activity that you may be doing. We would encourage you to keep practising on a regular basis, at least a couple of times a day – even for a few minutes at a time. That way you'll be strengthening your skill of being in the present moment. We have included a few further mindfulness exercises here that we would encourage you to practise now, before you read on, and to return to practising whenever you want. In the appendix we have included some other sources of mindfulness practice.

# Exercise 3.4

## Mindfulness of sight, sounds and touch

Throughout the day take a moment, wherever you are and whatever you are doing, to stop and notice your experiences with the following steps; take your time and do them one at a time.

- Take a look around you and notice three things (one at a time) that you can see.

- Listen to your surroundings and notice three sounds (one at a time) that you can hear; you might like to notice whether they are near or far ... and the silence between other noises too.

- Bring your attention to your body and notice three sensations (one at a time) that you can feel. You might notice the sensation of your watch against your wrist, air on your face, your feet against the floor or your back against your seat.

Whenever you become distracted, just notice the distraction and then gently, but deliberately, bring your awareness back to whatever sights, sounds and sensations you are noticing within that moment.

## Exercise 3.5

### Mindfulness of your mobile phone

Instead of using your phone on autopilot, try to bring awareness to your experiences of it from time to time.

■ Try picking your phone up and noticing its weight in your hand. Acknowledge how your body is now one phone heavier.

- Notice any automatic urges to check your phone and instead just let these pass; there's no need to act on these, simply return your awareness to the weight of your phone in your hand.

- Look at your phone with curiosity and notice its markings, colour.

- Explore your phone with your fingers and notice its texture and its temperature against your skin.

- Notice any thoughts arising in your mind about your phone, about this exercise or anything else; allow these thoughts to come and go. There is no need to stop them or follow them, simply return your awareness to noticing the sensations of the phone in your hand, again and again.

- When you are ready to put your phone down, you can take a moment to acknowledge how your body is one phone lighter.

## Exercise 3.6
### Mindfulness of brushing your teeth

Practising mindfulness of everyday simple activities that
we usually do on autopilot can be a great way to cultivate
your present moment awareness. You might like to use your
non-dominant hand (or whichever hand you tend not to use
when brushing your teeth) to really become aware of your
experiences.

- Pick up your toothbrush and notice its weight in your
  hand.

- Squeeze some toothpaste onto your toothbrush, notice
  the amount of pressure from your fingers needed to do
  this and then, with curiosity, take a moment to notice
  its colour, texture, smell.

■ Begin to brush your teeth, notice the movements of your arm and hand. Notice the sounds coming from your mouth.

■ Notice any urges to swallow or spit before you swallow or spit.

■ Rinse the toothpaste from your mouth with water, carefully listening to the sound of water swirling around your mouth.

■ Acknowledge the urge to spit and allow that urge to flow through you, before you do so.

Should any thoughts (about the exercise or otherwise) or any feelings (such as restlessness or boredom) take your attention away from the experiences of brushing your teeth, just acknowledge these thoughts and feelings before gently returning your awareness to the experience of brushing your teeth, again and again.

## Introducing yourself to yourselves

At the start of this chapter we introduced the idea that when we're on autopilot mode we tend to be automatically driven through life by our thoughts or emotions. We become used to treating our thoughts and other internal experiences very seriously as if they are facts, truths or commands that must be followed. In the context of our evolutionary history, listening to the contents of our minds is a very helpful thing to do. Doing so helps us to think, analyse and problem-solve our way through the vast majority of challenges and threats we encounter – we'll discuss this in more detail in the 'Loosen up!' chapter. We have also discussed times when being driven through life by our thoughts or emotions might not be so helpful.

It's worth noting that during the mindfulness exercises covered earlier you were doing something that no other species on the planet is thought to be able to do: a part of you was thinking those thoughts, feeling those feelings and sensing those sensations; however, there was also a part of you that was *noticing* and *observing* you thinking thoughts, feeling emotions and sensing sensations.

In ACT we differentiate between our **thinking self** and our **observer self**. These are two very different perspectives from which you can experience yourself and the world around you. You may be very familiar with the first perspective (the thinking self) and perhaps less familiar with the second (the observer self). In fact, there may be a perspective of yourself that you have not connected with for a very long time, even though it has been with you since you were very young. To see what we mean by this, try the following exercise.

## Exercise 3.7

### Look up at the sky

If you are able to right now, look up at the sky and take note of everything you can see. If you can't look up at the sky right now, then just take a moment to imagine what you'd see if you did.

The chances are that you are noticing (or imagining) clouds, birds, aeroplanes, the sun, darkness, the moon, stars or rain.

It's very common for us all to notice the *contents* of the sky (what's passing through it at a given moment) but to lose sight of the actual sky itself – the space that *contains* these various elements. Did you find that you did that too?

Just like the sky, our *observer self* is always there, always present and seems to have room for any of the emotions or thoughts that pass through it. However, when we experience strong emotions or unwanted thoughts, we often lose sight of our observer self and instead see only our thoughts, feelings and sensations (our *thinking self*). We then assume that these thoughts and emotions are *us*; that in a given moment these thoughts and emotions are all we are, rather than experiences that happen to be passing through us within a given moment.

It can be helpful to remember that the sky is never overwhelmed by even the fiercest weather conditions; there is always enough space for even the biggest storm or the strongest hurricane. Just like the sky, the observer perspective is never overwhelmed by even the strongest emotions or most difficult thoughts – there is always enough space. It's always there, yet sometimes we forget to see it. What's more, sooner or later the weather changes ...

It's important to acknowledge that this notion of two 'selves' is a rather abstract concept! Let's take a look at these two different perspectives from which we can view ourselves in more detail, one at a time. Let's first take a look at the *thinking self*.

### Your thinking self

You are probably very familiar with this perspective on yourself. Your thinking self is made up of *all* the ideas you have about yourself that contribute to your sense of self-identity. Your thinking self is comprised of all your thoughts, feelings, physical sensations, memories, rules, judgements and descriptions about yourself, others and the world. Other words for your thinking self might include your self-concept or 'who you think you are'.

You can tap into your thinking self by completing the following exercise; give it a go before you read on.

## Exercise 3.8
### Who am I?

We would like you to complete the following six statements.
There are no right or wrong answers. It doesn't matter
whether these ideas are 'true' or if they fail to encompass
every aspect of who you are. Simply complete the sentences
with whatever words (positive or negative) your mind
comes up with when you think about yourself. You can do
this exercise in your mind, or you might like to complete
these sentences by writing them down somewhere.

Introduce yourself ...

I am ...

I am ...

I am ...

I am ...

I am ...

I am ...

What kinds of words has your mind used to complete these sentences about yourself? Perhaps some positive words, such as 'I'm friendly'; perhaps some negative words, such as 'I'm boring'; perhaps some words that seem benign or purely descriptive, such as 'I am a son/daughter'.

Whatever you have written, this is a good example of your thinking self in action.

Your thinking self is excellent at providing stories about you, other people and the world around you. It is a really helpful tool that allows us to communicate, predict and plan future events, solve complex problems and learn from the past. However, listening to and then following all the stories it gives us can be really problematic at times, particularly when buying into those stories gets in the way of the kind of life we'd prefer to be living. For example, we can get caught up in stories about:

- **the past or future**: 'I'm bound to fail at that'; 'I shouldn't have done that'

- **the self**: 'I am so boring/ugly/stupid/useless'; 'other people are much better than me at that'

- **rules**: 'I can't show people that I am anxious, they will judge me as weak'; 'I need a partner to be happy in life'; 'I have to feel 100% confident before I do that'; 'I need to do it perfectly'.

Your thinking self is a skilled storyteller and is busy telling you these stories all day long. Some of these stories may be true to a degree, but often they don't reflect the whole truth. They may also be an expression of opinion or evaluation, rather than factual statements. To see what we mean, have a think through this concept with the following scenario.

## The comfy chair versus the uncomfortable chair
### (adapted from Hayes et al. 1999)

Suppose you were sitting on a green chair and we asked you to describe that chair. You might say that the chair was green, and we would of course agree with you. Say, however, that you went on to describe the chair as comfy. We might disagree and insist that actually the chair is really uncomfortable. So, we all agree on the colour of the chair but disagree on whether it is comfortable or not. How can this be? How can the chair be both comfy and uncomfortable?

Well, when we all agree that the chair is green we are observing and describing the actual colour of the chair, just as it is. But what is the difference between this and describing the chair as comfy or not? Where does the comfortable-ness or uncomfortable-ness of the chair exist? Is it in the actual chair or somewhere else? In essence, rather than describing the chair as it is, when talking about the chair being comfortable or uncomfortable we are instead evaluating the chair. These evaluations of the chair can differ because we are not actually describing the chair but saying something about *our reactions* to it.

Now, suppose that you rated yourself as 'boring/ugly/useless', etc. Is that a factual description of you or an evaluation of yourself? What do you think? Could you also say '*I am a human being and right now I am having an evaluation of myself as boring/ugly/useless*'?

Consider what might happen if you continued to buy into that evaluation of yourself, as if it was a factual description of what you actually *are*. How might it affect your confidence in social situations? How might your behaviour be affected? Perhaps you would avoid speaking up when you were out socialising with friends, or even avoid social interactions altogether, even if socialising still mattered to you.

Just like the chair being comfortable or not, ratings and evaluations of yourself are not *you*, but are your thinking self at work. Our *evaluations* can change, without the actual thing we are evaluating changing.

It's important to note that in the exercise above we're not trying to suggest that our descriptions are 'true' or 'right' and evaluations are 'wrong', nor are we necessarily encouraging you to 'change' your evaluations. We're simply re-emphasising the importance of noticing the difference between the two, because that's something our minds often forget to do.

As we can see from the above exercise, listening to these products of the thinking self on autopilot and using them to guide our behaviour can be quite problematic at times. Getting caught up in these stories can cause us great distress and impact upon our behaviour to such an extent that we may find ourselves no longer living life in the way that we might wish to. Try the following exercise to remind yourself of the impact that buying into thoughts can have on your experience, behaviours and life in general.

## Exercise 3.9
### Lemon squeezy

For the next couple of minutes (once you have read through these instructions) please close your eyes and really think about a lemon. Try to bring a lemon to mind, notice its vibrant colour, shape, texture of its skin. Once you have a vivid picture of a lemon in mind, imagine sniffing its skin – see if you can notice any citric scent. Next, imagine grasping the lemon firmly between your two hands and ripping it into two halves, noticing the juice squirt out and down your wrists. Next, imagine taking a deep bite into one half of the lemon and imagine its sour taste along with the sensation of juice dripping down onto your chin ...

OK, once you have done that please return to the rest of this exercise.

The chances are that during the above part of the exercise you might have noticed the smell and taste of a lemon and its juice (maybe slightly, maybe strongly!) as you were running through the instructions in your mind. You may even have felt a rush of saliva or a feeling of disgust (assuming you don't like the taste) or a pleasant feeling (if you do!).

This exercise shows us that even without actually having a lemon, simply 'buying into' thoughts about a lemon can create a consequential experience. With this point in mind, consider what might happen if you replaced the lemon with:

- stories about your past mistakes, regrets and 'if onlys'

- images and memories of a traumatic incident you might have endured

- harsh judgements about yourself

- your imagined future with all its looming problems.

The chances are that if you gave all these products of your mind the same kind of attention as you did the lemon, not only might you feel distressed but you might also begin to allow these thoughts to affect your life in ways that don't seem helpful.

It's important to remind yourself that the lemon was not actually there! Just as the lemon was not actually there, perhaps your thoughts – *'I'm useless/fat/ugly/useless'*; *'He/She is better/cleverer/more attractive than me'*; *'I can't do this or that'* – may also be describing things that are not actually there.

The sad reality is that, as human beings, we are likely to suffer unduly if we remain on autopilot and allow our thinking self to lead us through life. Our thinking self can create idealised futures that we long for, it can evaluate and form negative opinions about ourselves and others and construct all kinds of unhelpful thoughts, all of which can cause us further suffering.

Last, but by no means least, is the thinking self's ability to pull us away from the present moment. We can become wrapped up in the contents of our thoughts in a way that leads us to lose contact with the present moment and everything it offers. If you are on board with this idea, you may be starting to appreciate the limitations of your own thinking self and how continuing to listen to the products of your mind (thought and language) on autopilot may at times actually lead you *away* from living the kind of life that really matters to you.

So, how do we free ourselves from our thinking self? Well, the mindfulness exercises already described in this chapter will help you with that to some degree, as well as some of the other practical tools still to come in the next chapter. However, you'll also need to learn more about your *observer self*, so let's take a closer look at that right now.

### Your observer self

As we said earlier, your observer self is similar to the sky; always there, always present, even though most of us lose sight of it for much of the time. There are no thoughts occurring in your observer self, as they only crop up in your thinking self. To help

you understand your observer self, you might like to think of it as
the part of you that can simply *notice*, *acknowledge* or *watch* your
experience (thoughts, feelings, sensations) and the events in
the world around you; nothing more than that. Try the following
exercise to explore this idea.

## Exercise 3.10
### Just this book

Just take a moment now to observe and notice the book you
are reading. Whether in a hard copy held in your hands or an
electronic version on your tablet/laptop, just take a moment
to acknowledge it (and do nothing more than that). Now,
the chances are that, as you do this, it may be only a matter
of seconds before your thinking self pipes up with thoughts
and stories about the book or the exercise you are doing
right now. Maybe your thinking self is giving you opinions,
judgements or preferences ('*What do they want me to do?*',
'*This is a waste of time*', '*This seems really helpful*', etc.). These
thoughts are compelling and pull on our attention. It doesn't

take long before we become caught up in them as more and more thoughts rush to the forefront of our mind. So, instead of simply observing this book as you intended to at the start of this exercise, all the chatter of your thinking self is now taking centre stage!

Now consider how this experience might apply to any unwanted feeling you might have. For example, let's say you felt anxious. Simply observing this unpleasant emotion would result in *just this feeling called anxiety*. However, in most cases, our thinking self pipes up and begins to reel off a series of judgements, evaluations, preferences and predictions about that emotion, such as '*I hate feeling this way!*', '*Why is this happening to me?*', '*There must be something wrong with me!*', '*What if it never stops?*', '*I can't cope!*', '*I'm going to have a heart attack!*', '*I need to get out of here!*' Now what do you think would happen if you were to automatically listen to all this chatter of the thinking self? It's likely that your anxious feeling would increase, or even turn into a full-blown panic attack, in no time at all.

Instead, taking an observer self perspective on our experiences means that we are adopting a kind of 'hands off' approach, just continuously watching and observing, nothing more or less than that.

Just like the sky, your observer self is the continuous YOU. Unlike thoughts, emotions and physical sensations, your observer self remains constant, unchanging and stable. Dropping into your observer self can be a really helpful perspective to take and can free us up from the (often distress-inducing and life-limiting) stories of the thinking self. From the observer self perspective, we can notice and watch the stories that our thinking self is generating, without becoming caught up in them.

Your observer self is greater, larger and more expansive than your thinking self, it is the part of you that you call 'I'. YOU are bigger and more than your thoughts and feelings. Your observer self is the space from which you can stand and observe the stories that your thinking self is producing.

We have already mentioned how you might consider the observer self as being much like the sky (while your thinking self is like the weather that passes through it). Another way of looking at this is to reflect on how the observer self is like a chessboard, as in the following metaphor.

## Being more like a chessboard
### (adapted from Hayes et al. 1999)

Getting caught up in a struggle with your thoughts and feelings is much like being pulled into a game of chess. Consider how all your negative thoughts and feelings are like the black pieces on the board, and all your positive thoughts and feelings are like the white ones. Now, each time your mind gives you a negative thought or feeling (such as '*I am boring/useless/ugly*') and you feel sad or anxious, you instinctively try to fight back by moving a white piece forward that says

*'No I'm not, I'm funny, intelligent and attractive'*. However, it's important to remember that white pieces attract black pieces (and vice versa), so it's only a matter of time before another black piece charges forward again to remind you of how disliked you are and you feel sad and anxious once again. Trying to dominate the board with white pieces is common to us all, and maybe this battle resonates with you too?

The problem is that this is no ordinary game of chess. The board extends in all directions and there are an infinite number of white and black pieces – this fight never ends! It's time-consuming, energy-zapping and gets in the way of the life we might prefer to be living if we weren't caught up in such a futile fight. What's more, there's only one loser because the white and black pieces are both *yours*!

But who are *you* really? The black pieces are yours ... and the white pieces are yours ... but what part of this metaphor are *you*? What if you could be the chessboard – the strong, stable structure that holds all the pieces? This is where the observer self comes in. The chessboard itself is not involved in this endless battle. Maybe we can be more like the board, allowing us to step back and observe our thoughts and feelings, allowing them to come and go, to flow through us, as we refrain from getting involved in this fight. This way we retain the energy, time and effort required to create the life that really matters to us instead.

In order to be like the chessboard as described above, we can practise taking this observer perspective upon our experience. The mindfulness exercises already covered earlier in this chapter will help with this for sure, and you might also like to continue to practise contacting your observer self through the exercises that follow.

## Exercise 3.11

### Practising an observer perspective

Please don't rush through the steps in this exercise. Give yourself a couple of minutes to work your way through each one, one at a time.

- Can you notice that the air is a bit cooler as you breathe in and a bit warmer as you breathe out ... and then notice that there's a part of you doing the noticing?

- Can you notice any thoughts that are running through your mind right now ... and then notice that there's a part of you doing the noticing?

- Can you notice any physical sensations you're experiencing right now ... perhaps touch, heat or pressure ... and then notice that there's a part of you doing the noticing?

- Can you notice any images or memories that are in your mind right now ... and then notice that there's a part of you doing the noticing?

- Can you notice any sounds around you right now ... and then notice that there's a part of you doing the noticing?

- Can you notice any emotions that you're experiencing right now ... and then notice that there's a part of you doing the noticing?

- Just reflect for a second on who is doing all this noticing. Yes, that's right, it's YOU. So, there's a part of you that *notices* everything that you can see, hear, smell, touch, taste, feel, think and do.

- Notice that if you can notice these experiences, you cannot also *be* these experiences.

- Notice that this part of you that is just noticing is neither good nor bad ... It just *is*.

The above exercise is a great way to start making contact with your observer self. Hopefully, by trying it out, you have come to experience that there is a part of you that can notice and observe all of your other experiences. From this perspective you can notice how you are *more* than the thoughts, emotions and sensations you experience at a given moment. If you can notice this, you can give yourself the opportunity to *choose* how to respond to them.

This brings us back to the idea of the two paths at the start of this chapter. We can use the observer perspective to help us to *choose* how to respond to the thoughts and feelings we experience. When the way we respond moves us *towards* things that are important to us, we carry on. When the way we respond to thoughts and feelings moves us *away from* things that are important to us, we can respond a different way – more on what this might involve in the next chapter.

When you are ready, have a go at the next exercise to further explore your observer self.

## Exercise 3.12
### The continuous YOU

Once you have given this exercise a go a few times you might like to try it again with your eyes closed.

■ To begin, bring your attention to your breath. Notice the sensations of your breath being breathed by your body. Track each in-breath from the tip of your nostrils, down into your lungs, and then follow each out-breath as your lungs empty and your breath travels on its upwards journey out of the body. Continue to track your in- and out-breath in this way for a minute or so.

■ When you're ready, bring to mind a painful memory from when you were a child. Perhaps a time you had a nightmare or felt embarrassed at school, for instance. As this younger self, notice what worries are going through your mind, how you feel emotionally and physically, what you can see and hear. If you can notice those worries, feelings, sights and sounds, you cannot *be* those worries, feelings, sights and sounds. These worries, feelings, sights and sounds change but the YOU that notices them does not change, it never has. Notice that there is somebody behind the eyes of this younger self. Can you experience being this observer? What message would you like to send to this younger self about their suffering and their struggles with it?

■ Now bring to mind a painful memory from the more recent past. As this more recent self, notice what worries are going through your mind, how you feel emotionally and in your body, what you can see, hear. If you can notice these worries, feelings, sights and sounds, you cannot be these worries, feelings, sights and sounds. These worries, feelings, sights and sounds are constantly changing and there is still this YOU that notices them and does not change, it never has. Notice that there is somebody behind the eyes of this more recent self. Can you experience being this observer? What message would you like to send to this more recent self about their suffering and their struggles with it?

■ Now, notice what thoughts are going through your mind right now. Notice how you feel emotionally and in your body, what you can see and hear at this very moment. If you can notice these thoughts, feelings, sights and sounds, you cannot be these thoughts, feelings, sights and sounds. These thoughts, feelings, sights and sounds are constantly changing and there is still this YOU that notices them and does not change, it never has and never will. Notice that there is somebody behind your eyes noticing these experiences right now. Can you experience being this observer? This is the exact same observer that was present with your younger self and more recent self and will be again with your future self. What message would you like to send to yourself about any pain you may be suffering right now and your struggles with it?

In an exercise like the one above we can notice that the observer self is always present and continuous. It is there in each and every moment that you exist; it was present when memories were recorded in your past, it is here with you right now as you read this book and it will be with you as events continue to unfold (both internal and external to you) in your future. Unlike the constantly changing thoughts, feelings and sensations you experience and the ever-shifting world around you, your observer self remains the same, constant and unchanged. By adopting the perspective of the observer self we can experience a great sense of clarity and stability as we make contact with our experience of being more than our thoughts, feelings and sensations. The observer self has no agenda, judgements, regrets about the past or predications about the future. It is inherently present focused, compassionate and accepting. It is from this perspective that we can choose how to respond in the presence of difficult thoughts and feelings and behave in ways that help us to reduce our suffering and live life according to what matters most to us.

That is where this chapter ends. Hopefully you have a sense of what it would mean to *wake up* and are eager to read on. The ideas and exercises covered in this chapter are key to laying the foundations for the further ideas and techniques that we'll be sharing with you in the following chapters. So, when you are ready, please do read on – it's now time to *loosen up* and *step up*.

To conclude, here are some of the main ideas and learning points from this chapter.

## Chapter 3 summary points

- Responding on autopilot to our thoughts and feelings can sometimes make us feel worse and lead us away from the kind of life that we would prefer to be living.

- It can sometimes be helpful to switch off this autopilot tendency, so we can *choose* how we want to behave at a given moment.

- At times, our minds can 'time travel', evaluate and construct rules about our experience and the world around us, and can also be very rigid. Allowing these products of the mind to lead us through life can be both distressing and life-narrowing.

- Practising present-moment awareness with regular mindfulness exercises can help us to be present to our unfolding experiences moment-by-moment. Mindfulness practice enables us to become unstuck from stories about the past or the future and/or how life should be, and allows us to connect with opportunities within a given moment.

■ We can view ourselves and the world around us from two different perspectives: the *thinking self* and the *observer self*. The observer self is continuous, always present and provides us with a greater and wider perspective on our experiences. Tapping into the observer self can help us to be aware that we are not defined by our thoughts or feelings and therefore gives us choice about how we respond to them, rather than allowing them to control our lives when doing so seems unhelpful. The observer self opens up the possibility for us to live an enjoyable and more fulfilling life.

# 4 Loosen up!

In the previous chapter we were looking at how responding to our thoughts and feelings on a kind of psychological autopilot can sometimes drive us away from what we truly want to do. In these situations, it can sometimes be helpful to switch off this autopilot tendency and instead deliberately *notice* our thoughts, emotions and physical sensations unfolding, so we can *choose* to respond to them differently, in a more helpful way.

In this chapter we'll be looking at some different ways in which we can choose to respond to the thoughts and feelings we experience. We will be looking at what it means to psychologically and behaviourally **loosen up** around the thoughts and feelings we experience, in the interests of getting back on track and moving towards the kind of life we want to have. What do we actually mean by loosen up? Let's have a look at this by returning to the metaphor we first introduced at the end of Chapter 2.

## Navigating the obstacles along your chosen path

Imagine that you're cycling along a track one day and you reach a fork in the path. One way is the route you've taken on many occasions in the past and is a well-worn track. It's reasonably clear, with no significant obstacles, and you know where it takes you. If you were cycling on autopilot, you would automatically turn down this path without hesitation. The second track is overgrown, thick with brambles and full of potholes. You've never taken this path before and it looks like a difficult, menacing and arduous route. Which path would you choose?

Now, what if we told you that everything that's important to you, everything that you care about deeply in your life, lies along that second path? Now, which path would you choose?

By choosing to take the second path, you would be making a deliberate and purposeful decision to do something that brings you closer to what you really care about in life. Whether you're focusing on how you want to behave within important relationships, how you want to act at work, how you want to take care of yourself or how you want to live your life more broadly, this is where the second path would take you.

As you move along this second path, you might encounter brambles, potholes, rocks and bumps. There would be no way of cutting down all the brambles or moving all the rocks, at least not without having to stop your journey. Instead, you'd be choosing to encounter them, to have them crop up along the way as and when they will, as you purposefully travel along the second path towards everything you care about. Maybe you'd suffer some knocks, grazes or cuts – would you be willing to have those? Would you be willing to experience these unwanted obstacles while you travel towards what you really care about?

## Hitting the feel-good button

Before we take a look at how we can loosen up, let's first recap and remind ourselves of the struggles that we tend to get ourselves into and why it can be helpful to develop an alternative way of responding.

As we discussed in Chapter 2, we often assume that if we experience distressing thoughts, emotions and sensations, we need to change those thoughts and feelings if life is going to get better. We explored how this 'fix it' approach to psychological 'problems' reflects most people's understanding of what healthcare should aim to achieve, and often leads us to try to reduce, control or get rid of the unwanted thoughts and feelings we experience.

Most of us spend a lot of our time 'hitting the feel-good button' in life and then trying our best to keep it firmly pressed down. In Chapter 2, we asked you to consider the ways you have tried to do this. We strongly encourage you to return to your answers to Exercise 2.2 at this point (page 34), where we asked you to consider *anything* you have ever tried to do to avoid or get rid of unpleasant emotions, thoughts and physical sensations. This is a fundamental point in understanding how we can all become stuck in life, so, before reading on, please do take a moment or two to remind yourself of your experience of using these strategies and the consequences of doing so.

As you may have noticed from your own experience, these 'fix it' strategies can sometimes have costs. Avoiding certain anxiety-provoking people or situations can lead to life becoming narrower. Distraction can be difficult and reduces our ability to focus on what we're doing. Doing things to feel better can sometimes bring unwanted consequences, with drug or alcohol misuse being a sad example of this. So, although these control strategies can sometimes reduce unwanted emotions in the short term, they can often *increase* suffering in the longer term. As we saw with the 'don't think about chocolate' exercise in Chapter 2, when we try not to think about a worry this often evokes the worry. When we don't want to feel anxious, not feeling anxious in itself becomes something to feel anxious about. If we try to avoid feeling depressed by staying in bed all day we can end up feeling even more depressed and hopeless by the evening.

Often, this understandable but problematic tendency to avoid negative thoughts and emotions can leave people with more of the thoughts and emotions they were initially struggling with, AND a lot of extra suffering, too. As we suggested in Chapter 2, perhaps it's the case that if you're not willing to have these difficult thoughts and feelings, then you've probably already got them. Let's consider this in more detail by returning to John, who we first met in Chapter 3.

John had been out of work for a couple of months and was beginning to worry about ever finding another job. Quite understandably, every time he attended a job interview he became anxious. The night before his next interview John found himself lying in bed, kept awake by thoughts about every single job interview he'd 'failed' at in the past. His mind also provided him with a number of pessimistic predictions about the future – *'You'll screw it up'*, *'They'll think you're hopeless'*, *'They won't be interested in you'*. The next morning, after a night of very little sleep, John woke up feeling exhausted and decided to make a phone call to cancel his job interview arranged for later that day.

John's decision to cancel his job interview was an understandable attempt to avoid any further anxiety and feelings of failure. However, although his worry and the immediate feeling of anxiety about that day's interview was reduced, his anxiety about future interviews and his negative, unhelpful thoughts about his past performance and the future were exacerbated – what's more, he ALSO now experienced lots of extra suffering.

Along with the understandable and quite natural level of anxiety John continued to experience about attending job interviews, the more he avoided them and the more preoccupied by regret and worry he became. He also argued with his wife more when she pointed out that John always seemed distracted. John felt increasingly stuck in his career and no longer experienced any sense of reward from his working life. He also started to avoid seeing friends, because hearing about their achievements left John feeling even more like a failure, stuck and fed up. This led John to feel even more isolated and miserable.

## Struggling with natural emotional pain creates suffering

What about you? Specifically, what kinds of *emotional pain* do you experience? Sadness? Anger? Anxiety? Fear? In John's case, his emotional pain was an entirely natural and normal reaction to the current circumstances of his life. Perhaps, when all's considered, your emotional pain is entirely understandable too, given your current circumstances. Importantly, consider now the kinds of extra *suffering* that occurs when you try to reduce, remove, avoid or escape from this natural emotional pain. Please take a few moments to consider your own experience again. Like John, you may also notice that trying to rid yourself of entirely normal and natural emotional pain – although an understandable and very human response – may be causing you greater suffering in the longer run. Consider the metaphor in the box opposite as another way of exploring this.

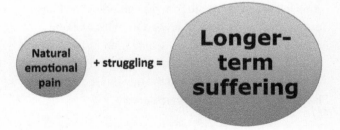

Natural emotional pain + struggling = Longer-term suffering

## Feeding your tiger!
### (adapted from Hayes, 2005)

Imagine that, after a long day, you get home and go into the kitchen to start cooking dinner. As you start cooking, you notice a kitten meowing and clamouring for your attention. In response, you give the kitten some milk from the fridge and this means he quietens down for the evening.

The next day you get home and once again find the kitten meowing, clawing at your ankle and trying to get your attention. Once again, you give the kitten some milk and he quietens down for the evening.

This pattern continues to occur each evening for the next few months. As time goes on, you start to notice the kitten growing bigger and each day he needs a bit more food before he'll quieten down. His meows are getting louder and his scratches are getting stronger.

Before long, you haven't got a kitten in your kitchen but a fully grown tiger! The tiger no longer meows, but roars and roars until you've given up everything in your fridge. Suddenly there's nothing left for you – everything has been lost, in the interests of subduing the tiger.

Does this bear any resemblance to your fight with threatening emotions? What have you given up in order to subdue these experiences? What have you lost? Have you got anything left to give?

### *Putting out fires*

To be clear: we do not mean to suggest that all avoidance of unwanted emotion always increases suffering or is somehow 'wrong' or 'bad'. As we said in Chapter 2, if avoiding snakes or other anxiety-provoking stimuli has no unwanted consequences and also allows someone to avoid feeling anxiety, then great! Sometimes though, as in John's case, when we respond to painful emotions by employing this 'autopilot' tendency to control or avoid, we begin to suffer more. As we can see, John felt increasingly stuck professionally, his relationship was starting to suffer and he no longer spent time with friends.

Different responses might work more or less effectively in different contexts. A bit like using water to put out a fire – it might work well most of the time but would not work so well if you were faced with an electrical fire. In this respect, the degree to which avoiding emotions (or responding in any other way for that matter) works in terms of allowing us to behave in a manner consistent with what matters to us depends entirely on the context in which we're applying the strategy. Rather than prescribing a rule that says avoidance is either 'good' or 'bad', 'right' or 'wrong', we encourage you to allow your experience to guide your decision making. When the way in which you respond to emotions leads you to behave in a manner consistent with the kind of person you want to be, then keep going – it's working! When your experience tells you it doesn't, try a different approach. When trying to control, avoid, reduce or eliminate our unwanted emotions increases our suffering, ACT offers a different approach.

We touched on this alternative approach at the end of Chapter 2. This alternative is called **willingness** and that's what 'loosening up', and the rest of this chapter, is all about.

*I'm having these really difficult thoughts, sensations and emotions,*

*AND*

*I'm willing to take them with me as I move towards the things that matter to me in life.*

## Increasing willingness

Willingness is all about being open to our whole experience, including our unwanted thoughts, emotions and physical sensations. If resisting thoughts or feelings and trying to control or get rid of them is not working well in terms of creating the kind of life we want to have, an alternative is to loosen up around them. In ACT, *acceptance* refers to our willingness to have all and any of these internal experiences (the good and the bad) that may show up as we move towards what we really care about in our lives. It's about experiencing all the emotions, sensations and thoughts that unfold within a given moment, without defence or judgement. Ongoing awareness of our thoughts and feelings requires a non-judgemental focus on the present moment, which is where the techniques described in the previous 'Wake up!' chapter are of enormous importance.

Willingness to experience all our thoughts and emotions in a given moment is a *choice* that we can all make throughout the day. It's something we *do* rather than something we feel; something we *do* in the interests of moving towards the kind of life we really want to have (more on this in the 'Step up!' chapter). If, in any given moment or context, our experience tells us that trying to control, change or avoid our thoughts and feelings takes us away from the kind of life that we want to be living, then it follows that accepting and loosening up around these unwanted thoughts and feelings, just as they are, might be a more useful strategy. It is often through our willingness to have and fully experience these thoughts and feelings that we can move closer to the life we'd prefer to be living.

It is important to note that willingness also has an 'all or nothing' quality to it – we can't really be a 'little bit willing' (again, more on this in the next chapter). It's like when you stand on the edge of a swimming pool, knowing that the water will be cold. Trying to get into the water and being a little bit willing to get wet will probably lead to a prolonged internal struggle with yourself and very little action – who knows whether you'll ever end up in the water or not. Willingness is much more like a two-footed leap into the water. This is a really important point, and the metaphor in the next box emphasises this in a slightly different way.

## The Transistor Radio
### (adapted from Hayes, 2005)

Imagine that you have an old transistor radio with two large dials on the front. One dial would usually adjust the volume and the other would be used to tune in to different radio stations. For now, let's imagine that instead of adjusting the volume or tuning, one of these dials measures the *strength* of your unwanted thoughts, emotions and sensations while the other dial measures your *willingness* to have and accept these experiences while you do things that move you towards living the kind of life that really matters to you.

As you go through life and come up against challenging situations it is highly likely that you will experience uncomfortable thoughts and feelings. The 'strength' dial might shoot up to level 5, 6, 7 or 8, maybe even 10. Where will your 'willingness' dial be set? How willing will you be to experience these thoughts, emotions or physical sensations?

Let's consider the possible answers to this question. What will happen if your 'willingness' dial is turned down low and you therefore try to control, avoid or eliminate these experiences? Consider how this might affect what you do, knock you off course and get in the way of you taking the challenging steps necessary to move you towards the life you want. Where does this leave you?

What if your 'willingness' dial were turned up high? Where would this leave you if the 'strength' dial got turned down low, or turned up high? If your 'willingness' dial was turned up high, could you continue doing things that matter to you, regardless of the strength of the unwanted thoughts, emotions and sensations you experience?

What's more, which of these two dials do you really have control over? Can you control the unwanted thoughts and feelings you experience, or would your efforts be better focused on cranking up the willingness dial to 10? Could you be totally accepting of these unwanted experiences and willing to have them? Can

you loosen up around them if doing so allows you to
move towards a more satisfying and meaningful life?

## What willingness is not

People often talk about 'confronting or facing your fear' or 'overcoming your anxiety'; to us, this implies clinging on for dear life as
you put yourself in a difficult or challenging emotional experience.
Willingness has a different quality to it; it's more of an *open*,
*accepting* and *curious* stance towards the emotions, sensations and
thoughts one experiences within a difficult situation. Rather than
tightening up in response to these unwanted experiences, it's all
about loosening up in their presence, and therefore allowing them to
come and go as they naturally will anyway.

Willingness is not a feeling. You don't have to feel willing in
order to *be* willing to experience unwanted, difficult feelings and
thoughts. It's also not about wanting certain thoughts or feelings
either. You do not need to *want* to feel or think something in order
to be willing to do so. The question is would you be willing to

experience these unwanted thoughts or feelings if doing so moved you forwards in life towards something that mattered to you?

Willingness is absolutely not about tolerance, resignation or giving up; these terms imply enduring and suffering. When we are *being willing* we are not 'biting our lip' or 'putting on a brave face' – this sounds a lot like trying to suppress or push our discomfort aside. Instead, willingness can be an empowering, vitalising stance towards our thoughts and feelings that acknowledges their presence as well as the counter-productive nature of struggling against them. Consider this further with the scenario in the box below.

### Tolerance versus willingness

Can you remember the last time you had an argument with someone you cared about? For the purposes of this example, let's say you would normally prefer to act in a loving, caring and patient manner towards this person.

However, during this argument you feel angry, indignant and impatient. An autopilot response in an attempt to get rid of these unwanted emotions might be to snap, say something hurtful or to storm out of the room.

Instead, you choose to stay in the room and not to snap. What would it be like to *tolerate* the emotions you're experiencing? Is remaining tight-lipped, fighting to keep a lid on what you're feeling, clenching your muscles with the effort of remaining calm and composed – perhaps still all caught up in ruminative thoughts about how annoying and wrong the other person is – just fuelling your anger even more? In this state, although you might not feel like it, you could still perhaps do something caring, loving or patient, couldn't you?

Alternatively, what would it be like to be *willing* to feel angry, indignant and impatient? Noticing the physical sensations in your body that accompany these emotions; watching the thoughts that spring to mind as they come and go; observing the emotions as they rise and fall; while doing something caring, loving or patient ...

*Being tolerant* and *being willing* might look quite similar to an outside observer most of the time ... but would look very different to you, the inside observer.

Tolerating our painful and unwanted experiences can feel stressful, lead to more (internal) suffering and at times regret and/or resentment about the actions we choose to take. So, with that in mind are you ready to develop true willingness?

Developing willingness might represent a very different way of responding to difficult thoughts, emotions and physical sensations. Particularly if you are someone who has tried to exert control or influence over these psychological experiences in the past, responding differently will be a big change.

The first step to loosening up is all about allowing difficult thoughts and feelings to be there, to pass through you, rather than trying to push them away. Exercise 4.1 provides an opportunity to practise this. Remember, willingness is something we *do* rather than feel or think. With that in mind, please have a go at the following exercise.

## Exercise 4.1

### It's not about feeling better, but getting better at feeling

This exercise is all about *feeling* emotions as they are, nothing more or less than that.

You might like to read through the following steps a few times before you start so you can focus on the exercise rather than trying to read at the same time. You may also find it helpful to close your eyes during the exercise, but that's totally up to you. Don't rush through this exercise, and give yourself at least a few minutes to work through each of the steps.

Throughout this exercise your mind is likely to wander, and that's entirely normal; there's no need to try to stop that from happening. Every time you notice that your mind has wandered, well done! You've given yourself the opportunity to gently escort your attention back to the exercise.

- Start by finding a comfortable position to sit or stand and take a few moments to get in touch with the physical sensations in your body, especially the sensations of touch or pressure where your body makes contact with your chair or the floor. Notice some of the physical sensations involved in taking a breath, including the rise and fall of your chest and the temperature of the air as it passes in and out of your nose and mouth. Simply allow these sensations to be as they are, without needing to change them in any way.

■ Now, gently shift your attention to something you're worried, afraid, angry or sad about. Notice any thoughts, worries, fears, doubts or unwanted physical sensations that might come along. As you notice these aspects of your experience, acknowledge their presence without becoming caught up in them, trying to work on them or change them in any way.

■ Continue to focus on this thought or on a situation that has been bothering you. Whatever emotions or physical sensations show up, simply shift your attention onto and into this discomfort with *curiosity*. Breathe alongside the discomfort. There is the discomfort and then there is you, breathing alongside it, allowing it to be there. There's nothing to be changed, no particular state to be achieved. Just stay with whatever you're experiencing.

■ If you notice yourself resisting, struggling against or trying to reduce the emotions or physical sensations you have, simply notice that tendency occurring and instead try to make some room for these experiences. Breathe alongside them; loosen up around them; open up to these feelings, make some room for them and allow them to be there.

■ Be as curious as you can and see if you can notice whether these emotions or physical sensations rise or fall, come in waves or stay the same. Just notice the changeable nature of these experiences. Allow them to come and go, as they naturally will, as you continue breathing and loosening up around them.

■ Allow these feelings to linger for a while as you curiously observe them. Remember: the purpose of this exercise is not to change these experiences in any way, but instead to make room for them, loosening up around them, allowing them to be there, just as they are.

■ Whenever you're ready to bring this exercise to an end, please do so.

We would encourage you to repeat this exercise regularly; especially when you notice any strong emotions (such as sadness, anger or anxiety) show up. Instead of struggling with these feelings, try responding to them differently, with *curiosity*. Remember: the purpose is not to get rid of the feelings but to loosen up around them, to increase your willingness to have them.

## Loosening up from thoughts

In the last chapter we asked you to spend some time deliberately watching your mind, noticing the constant stream of thoughts that occur as you engage in the process of thinking. The sheer number of thoughts that each of us experiences on a day-to-day basis (estimates range from 16,000 to 90,000; suffice to say, a LOT!) means that many of our thoughts pass us by without us really noticing. Some of our thoughts might seem hopeful, positive or pleasant to experience. However, particularly during a difficult period in life, our thoughts can become sad, frightening, angry and generally more difficult to experience.

Before thinking about how we can loosen up around the difficult, unhelpful thoughts we experience, it might be worth defining what exactly we mean by a 'thought'. This might seem unnecessary, but in our experience thoughts can be difficult to define.

Thoughts are things we say to ourselves (yep, that's correct we all do this, it's just that nobody talks about it). They tend to be sentences and more than one word. They can also be memories or images that flash into our minds. Our thoughts can exert enormous influence over what we feel and what we do. For example, if you passed an acquaintance in the street who didn't greet you, a thought might pop up along the lines of *'He's SO rude!'*, which might lead to a very different emotional and behavioural reaction to the thought *'He's clearly busy, he can't have noticed me'*. So, our thoughts *can* determine how we feel and what we do – *but they don't have to*.

We began this chapter by thinking about the assumption that if we have distressing or unhelpful thoughts, emotions or sensations, we need to change those thoughts and feelings if life is going to get better. This assumption reflects most people's understanding of psychology and you can find many, many self-help books that promise to help you think more positively and get rid of your doubts, worries and fears. Indeed, cognitive behavioural therapy (CBT – the most widely used psychological approach in the UK) helps people to challenge or dispute negative, counter-productive thoughts and replace them with more helpful alternatives, in order to help people feel better.

Changing the content of our thoughts can be a very helpful strategy, not least when we spot ourselves thinking in a way that is a less than accurate reflection of reality. Needless to say, we can all spot instances of ourselves thinking in a catastrophic, all-or-nothing or negatively charged fashion. What's more, we can all think of times when we've jumped to conclusions, generalised or taken things unduly personally. Certainly, a change of perspective in these situations can be helpful. We can all appreciate the value of thinking thoughts that seem more helpful, positive or rational, and there is a great deal of research to support this as an effective approach to psychological difficulties.

However, recent research challenges the assumption that changing the *content* of thoughts is necessary to help people prosper and achieve their goals. Indeed, changing our thoughts doesn't always seem to be necessary, which is a good thing, because often it can be very difficult to challenge the 'truthfulness' of thoughts. Sometimes difficult thoughts do reflect a difficult reality; no amount of thought challenging is going to change this. What's more, it can be difficult to challenge our thoughts within a given moment, and once we've managed to do so there's no guarantee we will actually *believe* the new thought!

Have you ever tried to argue with someone who thinks they're right? Consider your experience of doing so. It can almost seem as if, whatever you say, they've got a counter-argument at the ready. Our minds can be a lot like this – sometimes thoughts keep on coming, despite our best efforts to change them.

So, what are our options? Certainly, we can't simply suppress or stop these thoughts from occurring. That much should be clear from the 'don't think about chocolate' example in Exercise 2.5. The moment we try to stop thinking a particular thought, we're thinking it!

One option is to challenge the content of our thoughts and replace them with something more helpful. If your experience tells you that this allows you to behave in a manner consistent with the kind of person you want to be, it's surely a very helpful strategy. However, changing our thoughts is not the only option. There is an alternative.

So, how else could we respond to sad, frightening, angry or other difficult and unhelpful thoughts? Before looking at this in more detail, it's worth pausing to return once again to think in a little more detail about the nature of the human mind.

## How our minds work

One of the unique capabilities of the human mind is its ability to create *symbolic representations*. What do we mean by this? Well, every time we encounter a new experience, we create a representation of it in our minds and then make use of that representation later on. This allows us to think about things and experience them, beyond what we can see, hear, feel, taste or touch within a given moment.

For example, if we asked you to think about a nice cold glass of orange juice or a delicious lemon drizzle cake, you might get a rush of saliva. You may have experienced something similar to this in Exercise 3.10 ('Lemon Squeezy'). Thinking about seeing a loved one in a few weeks' time can make you feel excited. Recalling a particularly gruesome or shocking scene from your favourite television show can leave you feeling on edge as you try to fall asleep. In short, we can often react to an idea in our heads as if it were really happening in the here and now.

What's more, we don't only store these representations in our head and respond to them. We also create links between them. For example, if you knew that lemonade would taste the same as lemon drizzle cake, you would perhaps start to salivate at the thought of lemonade – regardless of whether you had ever tasted it before. If you learned that a film was even more violent than the television show you had previously watched, you might feel anxious about watching the film despite having never actually seen it.

This ability leads us to react to situations and ideas in our minds we have never actually experienced. This offers us enormous benefits, particularly as it enables us to solve problems and think our way out of difficulties that are not present at the moment.

This ability can also lead to problems, however. We become so good at creating representations in our minds and responding to them as if they are the real thing that we sometimes fail to realise that we are dealing with a representation rather than the real thing. For example, suddenly the thought '*I'm a failure*' can become confused with reality – we can start to listen (and respond to) this thought as if it's a truth or a fact. Similarly, thinking about something terrible happening to a loved one can sometimes seem as if thinking this thought increases the likelihood of something terrible really happening (even though we would probably all agree that thinking the thought *I'm going to win the lottery tonight* makes very little difference, unfortunately, to your chances of winning). In short, we can stop noticing the difference between our thoughts and reality.

This might not be such a problem, if it weren't for the tendency of our minds to think in such a negatively charged fashion. Maybe you find that your mind can become overrun with negative thoughts at times. It might be worth pausing for a second, to ask yourself which of the two different sets of thoughts in the next exercise resonates with you more strongly.

## Exercise 4.2
### Our threat-focused minds

Take a moment to consider which of the following sets of statements you can best relate to:

### Set 1

'I've done such a great job there.'

'What a fantastic boyfriend/girlfriend/wife/husband/friend/
employee/manager I've been recently.'

'I'm pretty sure it's going to work out as well as it possibly
could.'

### Set 2

'I really didn't do well enough there.'

'I've been letting people down recently.'

'It might work out, but there will no doubt be lots of
problems along the way.'

What did you notice? Most of us would probably recognise
these more negative, critical thoughts more readily. To
emphasise our point, perhaps you would be willing to try a
further brief experiment with the next exercise.

## Exercise 4.3 🚲
*Our critical minds*

Please spend a few moments looking around where you're
sitting/standing right now and see whether your mind can
evaluate everything around you in a negative fashion. Try
to find fault with everything you can see around you. You'll
probably find that your mind is pretty good at doing that!

Try that for a moment or two right now, before you read on.

How did you find that? The fact is that our minds have a great
tendency to evaluate things negatively. Why have we developed
this ability? As with every aspect of human development, the
answer is probably that it conferred enormous evolutionary
advantage.

Consider our first prehistoric ancestor who wasn't attentive to
sources of threat in his environment: he didn't anticipate danger,

didn't adopt a cautious approach to the outside world and wasn't on the lookout for predators; neither was he particularly aware of his shortcomings and didn't care much about the views or opinions of other tribe members. Now, consider whether he would have been more or less likely to survive than our second ancestor who was always looking out for threats: she anticipated threat and so always carried her spear; she was careful, always on high alert, thinking ahead to the next looming danger, primed ready for fight or flight. What's more, she was very aware of her shortcomings and physical limitations.

Clearly, the former ancestor was far less likely to survive than the latter. You, we and everyone else on the planet are the evolutionary product of those who were good at detecting and noticing threat – so over the years we've all become rather good at it.

However, on a typical walk to work or walk to the shops we rarely encounter threats such as lions, tigers or rival tribes. The threats we encounter in the modern world are of an entirely different nature. Shame, failure, vulnerability – these are threats of an entirely different nature and experiencing them wouldn't lead to our demise.

To summarise, our minds' ability to use symbolic representations means that we can sometimes fall into the trap of failing to adequately differentiate between the thoughts we think and actual reality. This can become problematic when we start to treat our thoughts as truths, facts, commands or premonitions (rather than *thoughts*), largely due to our minds' tendency to produce negative or threatening thoughts.

Let's return now to considering how we could respond differently to sad, frightening, angry or other difficult, upsetting and unhelpful thoughts?

## Looking *at* thoughts versus looking *through* thoughts

From the discussion above it's clear that as a result of our minds' best efforts to protect us from threat and danger, it can sometimes tell us things that are not entirely helpful. When we automatically listen to the content of our thoughts, see the world through our thoughts and allow our thoughts to drive our behaviour, we can often find that we move away from the life we'd prefer to be living and/or the person we'd prefer to be. Take a moment to notice what we mean here by having a go at the following exercise.

## Exercise 4.4

*Hands as thoughts*

*(adapted from Harris, 2009)*

For this exercise you'll need your hands to be free. First, have a read through of the following steps and, once you've read through them, please put your book down so that you can give the exercise a go.

- Imagine that you hands are your thoughts. Hold your hands open, palms facing up and together, so that your little fingers are touching each other at their tips. Hold them in this way, in front of you, as if they are the pages of an open book.

- Now, slowly and steadily raise your hands up, palms facing up, towards your face. Keep going until your hands are covering your eyes and touching the tip of your nose.

■ Take a look around you, peaking through the gaps of your fingers and notice how this affects your view of your surroundings. Is your view restricted? Are there things in your environment that you can no longer see? Consider what it would be like if you walked around all day like that. Would you miss out on anything? How would your actions be restricted? Could you do everything you wanted to do?

Now you can pick up your book again and, once you have read through the next steps, put your book down once more and give the following steps a go.

■ Hold your hands up to your face again, covering your eyes and touching the tip of your nose, as you did before. Now, this time, begin to lower your hands away from your face, very slowly.

■ As you do this, and as the distance between your hands and your face increases, notice how you are

able to connect to your surroundings once again and
take in more information about the here and now.
Notice how your visibility increases and with that how
you can more easily see and do the things that matter
most to you.

When we see the world through our thoughts, this can sometimes
restrict our view. Relating to the thoughts our minds produce as
facts, truths or something to be listened to is not always helpful.
Much like a friend who usually gives you sound advice, but
occasionally likes to wind you up, your mind can play tricks as
well! In these situations, we can choose to relate to our thoughts
in a slightly different way. We can look at our thoughts from a
different perspective, from which we can notice whether listening
to them is helpful or not in any given moment. One of the most
important steps in this process is to practise deliberately noticing
our thoughts *as thoughts*, as the following exercise describes.

## Exercise 4.5 🚲
### Noticing thoughts as THOUGHTS!

■ Take a moment to identify a particularly difficult thought – one that you often experience, perhaps about yourself, the world, other people or the future. It could be a fear, worry, doubt, criticism or regret that has a significant impact upon you when it shows up, for example, *'I'll screw it up'* or *'I'm such a failure'* (you might like to use one of the thoughts you listed in Exercise 2.1 for this).

■ Continue to *think* that thought for a little while, repeating it to yourself, noticing what happens when that thought really gets its teeth into you. Do you notice any physical sensations that come along with that thought? Do you notice any emotions showing up? Continue to allow that thought to get its grip on you for a little while, maybe 30 seconds or so.

- Next, carry on thinking that thought, but this time try repeating a specific phrase in front of it. The phrase is *'I notice I'm having the thought that ...'*; for example, *'I notice I'm having the thought that I'll screw it up.'* Repeat this a few times: *'I notice I'm having the thought that ... (insert your thought here)'*.

- Do you notice anything?

- Next, carry on thinking that thought, but this time, add a slightly different phrase in front of it. This time the phrase is *'I notice at the moment I'm having the thought that ...'*; for example, *'I notice at the moment I'm having the thought that I'll screw it up.'* Repeat this a few times: *'I notice at the moment I'm having the thought that ... (insert your thought here)'*.

- What (if anything) did you notice?

Sometimes, deliberately noticing a thought as a *thought* (as described in the third and fifth points in the exercise above) can have a surprising effect. People often describe experiencing a sense of distance between themselves and the thought. They may also notice a reduction in the strength, impact, grip or power of the thought. As we stand back and loosen up around the thought in this way, the impact of the thought somehow lessens, in a way that allows us to relate to the thought as ... well, a *thought*! An exercise like this allows us to notice that we are not our thoughts, nor do we *have* to relate to them as truths, facts, commands, premonitions or something that necessarily has to be taken seriously. Thoughts are ideas or opinions occurring suddenly in our minds – nothing more or less than that. They are simply products of the mind.

Importantly, we're not *changing* the content of our thoughts in any way with this exercise. We're simply helping ourselves to get better at relating to thoughts as thoughts in a way that can help us to respond to difficult thoughts in a more helpful manner. When it seems helpful to pay close attention to our thoughts, we can do so. When it seems more helpful to relate to our thoughts as what they are (i.e. just a thought), we can do so.

It is important to remember that these techniques are not designed to eradicate unwanted thoughts and/or to stop them from reoccurring. That sounds like trying not to think of chocolate again! The purpose of these techniques is to allow you to simply notice your thoughts in any given moment, in a way that allows you to loosen up around them. That way you have more choice over what you do next, rather than being driven around on autopilot by whatever thoughts you're experiencing.

Essentially, what we're doing here is looking *at* thoughts, rather than looking at the world *from* them. If you imagine your mind is like a computer system, capable of producing many, many different messages and electrical signals in any given moment, much of the time, we live life *thinking* these thoughts, almost as if our heads are *inside* the computer screen. These exercises are simply about gently lifting our heads out of the computer, so we can instead *watch* the messages as they appear on the screen.

## Freeing yourself from language traps

Sometimes certain words can become enormously powerful and have a significant influence on the way we feel and behave. As we explained previously, this is because we fail to differentiate between our minds' representations and reality. Take, for example, the case of Kristine.

Kristine had been troubled by thoughts about being a failure for many, many years. She usually managed to avoid these thoughts by working very hard at work and being careful to never, ever let anyone down. After a while though, this approach started to take its toll. Kristine felt exhausted and started making mistakes at work, which triggered enormously powerful thoughts about her being a failure and strong associated emotions. The more Kristine responded to her thoughts as facts (*'I'm such a failure'*, *'I must work harder'*, *'I mustn't let anyone down'*) and allowed them to direct her behaviour (i.e. working long hours, doing anything to please other people), the more tired she became and the more mistakes she made; the more she persisted to think of herself as a failure, the stronger her feeling of failure became.

Take a moment to consider whether you can relate to Kristine's experience. 'Failure' may not be something you struggle with, but you probably find that your mind comes up with descriptions about you that are painful to experience (other painful examples might include 'stupid', 'fat', 'weak', 'useless' or 'ugly'). See if you can boil those thoughts or ideas down to a word that encapsulates their collective meaning.

There are a number of techniques we can use to respond in a looser fashion to these kinds of negative, self-focused thoughts so they don't get such a strong hold over us and our behaviour. A useful starting point is to bear in mind that ironically, these words represent your mind's best efforts to protect you! After all, if you believe you're a failure and then feel all the associated emotions of failure, at least you'll never be caught off guard ever again by that thought and any of those scary emotions. Unfortunately though, these thoughts can sometimes also prove unhelpful, in which case the following exercises might be worth experimenting with.

Before continuing, we want first to acknowledge that some of these exercises can seem a bit strange or playful. You might start to wonder whether we are trivialising or underestimating the power of these words to cause you distress. That is absolutely not our purpose – we understand how painful these words can be. We have witnessed this in the clients we work with and experienced it first-hand ourselves. These exercises are all seeking to achieve a common purpose – to help people loosen up around these kinds of thoughts when it seems helpful to do so. Do please practise these exercises, so that you can start to figure out which work best for you.

## Exercise 4.6
### Playing with words

- To begin this exercise, please bring to mind a word you use to describe yourself and which you find painful. Examples might include 'failure', 'useless', 'ugly', 'fat', 'stupid' or 'unlovable'. These are just examples of course – we all have our different areas of vulnerability.

- Spend a few moments noticing how that word affects you. What does it make you feel, do or not do?

- Next, we would like you to say that word (aloud or silently if you wish) **verrrry sloowwwly** ... As you do this, do you notice any loosening?

■ Alternatively, try repeating that word rapidly (again silently if you wish) over and over again for 30 seconds ... does anything happen in terms of the impact of that word?

■ Or try singing that word to yourself to your favourite tune. For example, to the tune of Happy Birthday! Does anything happen in terms of the impact of that word?

You may have found that some of the techniques in the exercise above somehow changed or *loosened* the way in which you experienced that word. When we say these words slowly or repeat them rapidly we can notice them more as a sound (which is really what a thought is – a collection of words or sounds in the mind) and they tend to loosen in their meaning or impact. In this way, sometimes these *loosening up* exercises can help us gain a sense of a word as *a word* and a thought as *a thought*, rather than something that necessarily needs to wield such enormous power over what we feel and what we do. If you got a sense that the power of the word was loosening in any way, then you're having the kind of experience we are hoping to convey. If not, that's absolutely fine too. Changing the way we relate to thoughts and words can take some practice, particularly when those thoughts and words and their associated emotional impact have been rehearsed for such a long time. In addition, different exercises work for different people. We encourage you to keep practising the techniques from the last exercise and see how you go.

To return to the case of Kristine, she found these strategies helped her relate to 'failure' as what it is – i.e. a strange collection of sounds (or symbols on a page) which her mind produced. Kristine's learning history meant that she had begun to associate this sound with enormous importance about herself. Consider though what it would be like for Kristine to think the sound '*échec*', '*ausfall*' or '败'. Each of these words (or collections of symbols) might carry similar power for Kristine had she grown up in France, Germany or Japan respectively; however, because of her learning history, it just so happened that the sound 'f-a-i-l-u-r-e' carried much more meaning than any of these other sounds. However, it didn't have to!

## Getting some further distance from thoughts

Sometimes, when we are trapped by our inner dialogue, thoughts move so quickly that it can be difficult to notice them as *thoughts*

– instead, they are typically viewed as a reflection of reality. One way of thinking about this is to imagine standing on the edge of a platform as a train rushes past. It can be difficult to see the train because it's moving so fast – instead all you can see is a blurred rush of light. Stepping back from the platform edge can help you to see the train itself as it rushes past you; indeed, the farther back you are, the slower the train appears to travel.

Thoughts can be like this, too. When we are trapped in the never-ending content of our minds, it can be very difficult to see what those thoughts are. The following exercise is all about taking a step back from thoughts.

## Exercise 4.7
### Watching thoughts float by

This is an imagery exercise, so it might be helpful to do this somewhere where you can safely close your eyes. Take a moment to read through these instructions first before going ahead with the exercise.

■ Imagine one day you are up in the mountains, sitting next to a stream. The exact setting is not important, but imagine that you are sitting next to a stream and watching the water flow slowly past.

■ Every time you notice a thought, imagine gently placing it on a leaf and watch it float slowly past you. It's likely that your mind will wander during this exercise – that is normal and to be expected. Nevertheless, every time you notice a thought, place it on a leaf and watch it float slowly past you.

■ You might find that some thoughts seem difficult to experience, in which case you might notice a tendency to try to push these thoughts away down the stream. If this occurs, instead focus on watching that thought on its leaf as it floats gently past you.

■ For about five minutes, continue to focus on noticing your thoughts as each one shows up; whatever they are or happen to be about, place them gently on a leaf and watch them float slowly past you.

How did you find that exercise? Please take a few moments to reflect on your experience. You may have been struck by how quickly and automatically thoughts can come! Perhaps it left you with an insight into how easy it can be to forget that you're thinking, instead being wrapped up and bossed around by whatever thought your mind is generating within a given moment.

What was it like to notice thoughts, rather than getting carried away by thinking them? Whatever your experience, we're glad you had a go and congratulations for *noticing* whatever you noticed. Increasing your awareness of the process of thinking was the aim, after all, nothing more than that. It's important to note however, that virtually nobody would ever be able to place every thought on a leaf without getting distracted from the process! Our minds are very good at encouraging us to think rather than see our thoughts – could it be that at least some of these thoughts aren't what they claim to be? We hope by now that you are wondering whether this might be the case.

*I used to think that the brain was the most wonderful organ in my body. Then I realised who was telling me this...'*

*– Emo Philips*

As we mentioned earlier, when we were describing what thoughts were or looked like, verbal thoughts are not the only type we encounter. Sometimes people experience images or memories, which can be enormously powerful. Particularly if our minds start to confuse these images as a premonition or an entirely accurate reflection of the future, then these images can become extremely threatening and difficult to experience in their own right.

Spend a moment considering whether you struggle with any worst-case scenario-type images. These might include memories of a situation in which you felt frightened, or imagined scenarios in the future; for example, imagining seeing yourself or a loved one very ill. These are just examples, of course, and any unwanted images you experience may be entirely different. The following exercise describes an approach for dealing with these images when they show up. It's important to acknowledge that many of the images we experience can be incredibly painful to think about, and we certainly hope that the following exercise, which is a bit playful in nature, doesn't seem to undermine or underestimate the seriousness and painful nature of some of the images that enter your mind. Rather, we include these exercises because we hope they can offer you a means of loosening up around these images when they enter your awareness, if and when it seems helpful to do so.

## Exercise 4.8

### The cinema screen

- Bring to mind an image that you find very difficult to experience. Spend a few moments thinking about that image and noticing the emotions and associated physical sensations that may accompany that image.

- Holding that image in mind, imagine throwing it up onto a large cinema screen, and you are sat in the front row looking up at it. Now, let's experiment with a few techniques. First of all, imagine introducing a new element to that image. For example, notice what happens if you introduce a fictional character into the image.

- Alternatively, try adding a colour filter to that image so the image becomes florescent pink, green or perhaps black and white. The colour doesn't matter of course, we're just experimenting with whatever helps you to loosen up around that image.

■ Try zooming into a very small, pixellated aspect of that image. What's it like to reduce that image to a very small dot or, alternatively, magnify it until it's absolutely huge?

■ When you're ready to bring this exercise to an end, spend a few moments reflecting on whether any of those techniques helped you to loosen up around this image. In other words, were you able to allow that image to be there, rather than try to push it away or block it out somehow, as you might usually?

We hope that some of the ideas in this chapter may help you to *loosen up* around the thoughts, emotions and sensations you experience, when it seems helpful to do so. When the way you respond to thoughts and feelings takes you towards the kind of life you want to have or leads you to behave in a manner consistent with the kind of person you wish to be, there's no need to make any changes. However, when the way you respond to thoughts and feelings takes you away from these important things, the strategies and techniques in this chapter may prove helpful to you.

What works for you will be a case of trial and error. Please do experiment with these different ideas, practise them for a few weeks and then consider how well they are working. Remember, how well they are working is defined by whether they take you towards the kind of life you wish to have, rather than by whether they reduce the unwanted thoughts and feelings you're experiencing. This is a really key point. When we start to use the strategies described in this chapter to feel better, we then fall into the trap of trying to fix thoughts and feelings again, which, as we've seen, can sometimes be problematic.

In the next chapter, we'll be looking at how we know whether the way we are responding to any of our unwanted psychological experiences is working. This depends entirely on whether our responses move us towards or away from what truly matters to us, i.e. our *values*. So, once you've had a read through of the summary points for this chapter, its time to *step up*.

## Chapter 4 summary points

■ Most of us assume that if we experience distressing or unhelpful thoughts and feelings, we need to change those thoughts and feelings first if life is going to get better.

■ Trying to avoid or change unwanted emotions sometimes doesn't work so well and can lead people to suffer even more. In these situations, *willingness* is an alternative strategy.

■ Willingness is all about *loosening up* around our whole experience, including our thoughts, emotions and physical sensations; it is about taking an open and curious stance towards any upsetting thoughts and uncomfortable feelings we experience. This takes practice and is something we *do* rather than something we *feel*.

■ We all become very used to listening to our thoughts as if they are a truth, fact, command or premonition.

This can sometimes become unhelpful, particularly when it comes to difficult or unpleasant thoughts.

■ When we experience these thoughts, we can try to develop a sense of psychological distance from them. This can be helpful when it allows us to respond to these thoughts more effectively, in a way that moves us towards what we really care about in life.

# 5 Step up!

Throughout the book so far we've been exploring how being on autopilot means we often get automatically driven through life by our thoughts and emotions. We've been discussing how sometimes our struggles with unwanted thoughts and emotions can increase our suffering and take us off-track in terms of the life we'd prefer to be living. It can therefore sometimes be helpful to *wake up* and switch off the autopilot in a way that increases the scope for choice. Instead of being driven through life by our thoughts or emotions, we can instead *choose* what we want to do. This doesn't require us to get rid of these unwanted thoughts or feelings, but instead to *loosen up* around them; to increase our willingness to have them, and to actively and purposely respond to them in a more open and accepting way, without judgement, avoidance and defence.

In doing so we can free ourselves to focus on living the kind of life that really matters to us. Our stance towards life really does become:

*I'm having these really difficult thoughts, sensations and emotions,*
*AND*
*I'm willing to take them with me*
*so that I can move towards the things that matter most to me in life.*

If thoughts and emotions don't always prove helpful in guiding us towards the life that we want, what is left? What can lead us through life in a more helpful way? The ideas in this chapter can help you increase your chances of living a rich, full and meaningful life, especially if you've found that being controlled by your thoughts and feelings has led life to become narrow, limited or less meaningful. Specifically, we are going to encourage you to take a look at your *values* , i.e. what truly matters to you and what you really care about in your life. What would you choose your life to be about? What kind of person would you ideally choose to be? What contributes to your life being meaningful, fulfilling, purposeful and vibrant? What would *motivate* you to take the second and more challenging path in the following metaphor?

## What would make it worth choosing the second path?

Imagine that you're cycling along a track one day and you reach a fork in the path. One way is the route you've taken on many occasions in the past and is a well-worn track. It's reasonably clear with no significant obstacles and you know where it takes you. If you were cycling on autopilot, you would automatically turn down this path without hesitation. The second track is overgrown, thick with brambles and full of potholes. You've never taken this path before and it looks like a difficult, menacing and arduous route. Which path would you choose?

Now, what if we told you that everything that's important to you, everything you care about deeply in your life lies along that second path?

What would make it *worth* going along the second path? What do you truly care about that would lead you to step up to that challenge?

The title of this chapter, 'Step up!', was chosen deliberately. What does 'step up' mean to you? To us, it means actively and deliberately putting oneself forward for a difficult task. Choosing to accept a difficult road, perhaps involving some kind of pain or distress, in the service of moving towards something of great importance. By 'stepping up' we choose to listen to our hearts and move with our feet, rather than necessarily allowing our minds to direct our behaviour.

This chapter is, firstly, all about thinking about what you would choose for your life to be about. It's about identifying and clarifying what you really care about and value in life and using those fundamentally important ideas as a kind of beacon on the horizon, towards which everything else is directed. When the way we respond to difficult thoughts and unwanted emotions moves us towards that beacon, we keep on going. When our ways of responding move us away from what's important, we adjust our approach.

Once we clarify what we really value in life then it's all about taking action, in a committed way, ensuring that we behave consistently with our values while being accompanied by any unpleasant emotions, thoughts and sensations that may show up as we do so. Therefore, this chapter will also show you how you can begin to 'commit to putting your values into action'.

Taking some time to identify and clarify what really matters to each of us is extremely important, particularly given how easily obscured these fundamentally important values can become by the everyday hustle and bustle of our busy lives. Another way to think about this is given in the box below.

One way of thinking about life is to imagine a large glass jar. There is only so much room in this jar – it has a limited capacity and you can't fit everything in. Imagine that we asked you to consider what you most want your life to be about and to start by filling your jar with large rocks and stones, each of which represent one thing which is of fundamental importance to the kind of person you would choose to be and the kind of life you would choose to live. Imagine filling your jar with these large rocks until it seems as if there is no more space. Is it full?

Next, imagine taking a bag of smaller pebbles, which represent things you want in your life but don't have quite as much importance (for example, that job, increased salary, car, perfect body, etc). Fill your jar with these pebbles until it seems there is no more space. Is it full now?

Now imagine we gave you a bag of sand and asked you to pour sand into your jar, filling all the tiny spaces until it seems *completely* full. Is there any space left now?

Finally, take a jug of water and continue to fill the jar until the water reaches the top of the jar; now the jar is entirely full.

Sometimes, when we've been struggling with difficult emotions, unwanted thoughts or challenging physical symptoms, life seems to become entirely focused on our problems. Life can seem so overwhelmed, preoccupied, busy or distracted that we forget to focus on the things that really matter. This is a bit like allowing your jar to become full of water, sand and pebbles before you think about how to fit the big rocks in. When you get around to considering what contributes to your life being full, rich, meaningful and rewarding it can seem as though there's simply not enough space left.

## What are values?

Psychologists often talk about goals and values. Let's start by considering how we think about values from an ACT perspective.

Joanne Dahl and Steven Hayes have defined values as 'global, desired and chosen life directions'. They describe the qualities that we would prefer to demonstrate and bring to our actions in life on an ongoing basis. In other words, how we choose to behave, what we want to stand for and how we prefer to be as we go about our life, in our many different roles (i.e. as a partner, friend, parent, child, colleague, etc.) and within the many different situations we will encounter.

There are some important aspects of the definition above. Let's look at them one by one.

### *Values are freely chosen*

Firstly, values are the things you would *choose* for your life to be about. There are many expectations in life regarding the way we 'should' behave, often influenced by the expectations of others or society. Values are different; they are not what we *should* do or what others would like us to do, but instead what we *choose* to do. For example, if someone was taught from an early age the importance of being hard-working and therefore being lazy led that person to feel guilty and inadequate, they might well go through life working very hard. However, being hard-working wouldn't necessarily be one of their *chosen values* – they might instead work very hard in order to avoid feeling a sense of failure or guilt and to please others. Another way to think about your values is that they really wouldn't change, even if you never had to tell anyone what they were. They don't depend on other people's judgements.

Values also don't depend on responses from other people. If Bill resolved to be loyal towards his friends so that they would always maintain loyalty in return, this probably wouldn't really be a value.

On the other hand, if Bill resolved to be loyal towards his friends because this seemed like the kind of friend he really wanted to be (regardless of what others did), then loyalty might indeed be one of his chosen values. In this example, the 'reward' for being a loyal friend is intrinsic, rather than dependent on the responses of others. Of course, it's always nice for our deeds to be appreciated by other people, but true values will remain, even if there is nobody there to witness them.

Values are also not time-bound or dependent on particular situations. You can choose to act on your values whenever you want, irrespective of your life circumstances – there is no waiting involved when it comes to living by your values. For example, if Prina is single and not yet in a relationship but she still values being loving, she doesn't have to wait until she finds a partner before she can 'be loving' towards her friends, family, pets or herself. You are free to act on your values any time you choose.

### A value is a direction not a destination (or a goal)

Values give us a sense of *direction* in life, a bit like travelling east. If we continue travelling east we never really arrive at our destination, in much the same way that a value can never really be considered to be achieved or completed. For example, we never really 'complete' or 'tick off' being kind, hard-working or a loving parent, friend or partner. As we continue travelling along a valued path we may well encounter goals along the way, which of course can be achieved and completed. Similarly, as we move east we may encounter bridges that need to be crossed or hills that need to be climbed, but we never really arrive at 'east' – just as you would never finish or 'complete' being a loyal and loving friend.

These days, so many of us seem to live in a goal-focused way without consideration for what we truly value. Society often tells us to 'get this job', 'get that house', 'have a family', 'earn lots of money', 'have this kind of body', 'be happy', etc. Sometimes, this way of living life can become stressful and exhausting. Pursuing endless goals in the hope of gaining some sense of meaning or satisfaction in life may ultimately be unfulfilling. While we strive for the next goal we can feel that life is lacking in some way; in our single-minded pursuit of achieving the next goal we can end up missing out on other aspects of our life. Then, once we achieve the goal (if we ever do), we may feel anxious or lost and directionless about what to do next, so we then find ourselves seeking out the next goal. By contrast, living a 'values-driven life' means we can experience a sense of satisfaction in life, irrespective of whether we actually achieve our goals or not. Values are always present and they reside within us, not outside us; therefore they are always present to guide our actions and bring us a sense of meaning and purpose in life.

### *Values can be expressed in many different situations and many different ways*

Values are *global*. They inform how we choose to act in different circumstances and within different parts of our lives. They are also global in terms of our behaviour. A particular value can be expressed through many different actions. For example, someone who valued being a caring friend might express that value by choosing to give a friend some space or being sure to stand next to them in their time of need. Being a supportive and loving parent might sometimes involve being with a child, yet at other times might involve letting a child play and explore independently, or at other times by showing some tougher love! Valuing being conscientious and a hard worker might involve spending many hours at work, yet also knowing when the time has come to rest.

## What values are *not*

### *Values are not about being happy*

A life lived according to values is usually experienced as fulfilling, meaningful and rewarding, but this isn't always about feeling happy. In many ways this may make a lot of sense, particularly if you reflect on your own life.

If you take a moment to think back to everything you've ever felt proud of, you'll probably notice that some kind of pain or suffering was involved. Every time you enter into a relationship that matters to you, vulnerability and the possibility of loss, being hurt or left comes too. Every time you take on a great challenge, you accept the possibility of failing. Caring about your work can bring disappointment when things go wrong. In this way, it is important to recognise how pain and values really are poured from the same vessel. This important point is explored in more detail in the next exercise.

Indeed, just thinking about our values can sometimes lead us to feel upset, particularly if we realise that we seem far away from something of fundamental importance to the kind of person we would choose to be or the way we would choose to live our lives.

# Exercise 5.1
## The magic pills
### (adapted from Robert Zettle, 2007)

Imagine that we offered you some magic pills. Now, if you take these pills and have your closest friend or partner (delete as you wish) swallow them, we can guarantee you that they will always see and remember you as a loving and caring friend/partner for the rest of their lives, provided that you do just one other thing. The other thing that you must do in order for these pills to work is to ensure that you are as mean, uncaring and rude as you possibly can be to your friend/partner. In fact, the more mean, uncaring and rude you are to your friend/partner the more these pills will take effect and the more they will see you as loving and caring.

These pills are one option. We can call them 'Option A'. Now, instead of these pills you could choose 'Option B', which means that you can do away with the pills and instead commit to being as loving and caring to your friend/partner as you want. However, there is no guarantee that they will see you as a loving and caring friend/partner and in fact they may even grow to hate and despise you, leaving you feeling very hurt, depressed and anxious at times. In fact, despite how loving and caring you are to them, they may never see you that way, ever. Maybe they will, maybe they won't!

So, which option would you choose? What's more important to you? Being the kind of person you really want to be and doing what really matters to you in life, even if it feels uncomfortable or painful? OR, feeling safe and comfortable but also missing out on what truly matters to you in life?

Sometimes thinking about what we care about can be a very emotive experience. When we lose things that are important or spend less time doing things that matter, we simply feel bad. This is not necessarily an outcome to be avoided; indeed, if you notice feeling upset when exploring your values then it's a strong sign that you are probably hot on the trail of something that really matters to you.

### *Different values are not always compatible at any given time*

Sometimes values cannot all be serviced at the same time. You may be able to think about times in your own life when two values have conflicted. Someone who values honesty and loyalty might obscure the truth to protect a friend. Someone who values health and being a loving father might sometimes miss out on the gym for a few weeks to spend time with his children. Someone who values socialising and achievement might miss out on an evening with friends in order to meet an important deadline at work. Values cannot all be met at the same time, but this doesn't mean they are lost forever. It can sometimes be helpful to think of your values as attached to a spinning globe. Not each and every one of your values may be in full view in a given moment, but sooner or later they will spin back round towards the front of your attention.

### *Values are not 'right' or 'wrong'*

There are no 'right' or 'wrong' values from an ACT perspective – they just *are*. Different people will have different values. One person may value spontaneity, while another may value preparedness; one person may value independence, while another may value dependence. Neither is right nor wrong.

### *Values are not rules*

Values are not rules to live by. As we mentioned in the previous chapter, our minds can become very good at creating rigid rules for how we should live our lives, and this can sometimes reduce our ability to respond to a situation flexibly. To use some of the examples in the above paragraph, where would someone who valued honesty and loyalty be left if telling the truth left his good friend in trouble? How might our lives become narrow, rigid and limited if we valued being hard-working, conscientious and successful at all costs? Kelly Wilson, one of the founders of ACT, talks about holding values lightly and pursuing them vigorously, which is the best advice we can pass on to you, too.

## How to identify your values

There are a number of ways you can set about identifying your own personal values. As with anything, there is no right or wrong way – just do whatever works for you! We hope you might find the following exercises (Exercises 5.2–5.6) helpful in clarifying some of your own values.

The next exercises may feel slightly odd or unsettling to think about, but if you're willing to have a go we would encourage you to do so.

## Exercise 5.2

*It's a miracle!*

Imagine that a miracle has happened and tomorrow morning, when you wake up, you have achieved everything that matters to you in life. Imagine that you feel 100% confident and happy. You never have to prove yourself or impress anyone ever again and you can now do anything in life that you want to. With that in mind, consider:

- what will you do with your life?

- how will you act differently?

- how will you behave differently?

- how will you talk to yourself or others differently?

- what personal qualities will you demonstrate?

- what will others see that is different about you and how you are being?

## Exercise 5.3 🚲

How would you want to be remembered?

(adapted from Hayes et al 1999)

Consider what you might want to inscribed onto your headstone when your time on this planet is up. If we continue through life preoccupied with trying to control all our unwanted thoughts and feelings we can start to appreciate how our headstone might describe us with particular qualities and by certain actions that don't really reflect the kind of person that we truly want to be. For example, someone who feels anxious in social situations might avoid going out and meeting new people and therefore be described as 'solitary and preferring his own company' on his headstone, when actually he would prefer to describe himself as 'someone who values closeness, connection and belonging'.

How would you most like to be remembered?

Here lies
[your name]

S/He was a.......

[insert the qualities that
really matter to you,
i.e. courageous, loving,
fun, sociable etc]

person/partner/friend/parent

## Exercise 5.4 🚲

### Clarifying your most important values

Another way to uncover some of your values is to explore
the values listed opposite. Here are many different values
that people sometimes hold as important. Work through
the list, placing a tick next to any values you consider to be
important and a cross next to any you consider unimportant
(you might prefer to jot them down under the two different
headings, 'important' and 'unimportant' in your notes). You'll
probably find you have many values marked as 'important'
by the end of the exercise, so really think carefully about
what you consider to be of fundamental importance in your
life. Try to cut your 'important' list down by 50%, and then
cut it down again until you've identified your top ten values
(the precise number isn't important, but we encourage you
to be selective). Please note that your values can change
over time, so don't get too hung up on leaving out some of
your important values for now. You can always revisit this
exercise later on, review your values and create a new list.

| | | | |
|---|---|---|---|
| Acceptance | Adventure | Affection | Assertiveness |
| Attentiveness | Authenticity | Awareness | Beauty |
| Belonging | Caring | Challenge | Citizenship |
| Compassion | Communication | Conformity | Connection |
| Consideration | Contribution | Cooperation | Courage |
| Creativity | Curiosity | Dedication | Dependence |
| Devotion | Discipline | Diversity | Effort |
| Encouragement | Equality | Excitement | Experience |
| Expression | Fairness | Faith | Fitness |
| Flexibility | Forgiveness | Freedom | Friendliness |
| Fun | Generosity | Gratitude | Health |
| Honesty | Honour | Humility | Humour |
| Imagination | Independence | Integrity | Intimacy |
| Justice | Kindness | Knowledge | Leadership |
| Learning | Love | Loyalty | Mindfulness |
| Nurturing | Openness | Order | Organisation |
| Patience | Peace | Persistence | Play |
| Pleasure | Power | Productivity | Reliability |
| Respect | Responsibility | Risk | Security |
| Self-awareness | Self-control | Self-development | Sensuality |
| Sexuality | Skilfulness | Sociability | Spirituality |
| Spontaneity | Stability | Supportiveness | Thoughtfulness |
| Tolerance | Trust | Understanding | Warmth |
| Wisdom | Wonder | Work-ethic | Zealous |

It's really important to emphasise that this is not a complete list. There are many other values you may hold dear. What's more, the precise wording really doesn't matter. Sometimes words really don't adequately capture the essence of what really matters to us! If this is the case, we suggest just going with the words that best fit you (or make up your own); of greatest importance is that you know what you mean.

Your values probably show up in things you enjoy doing on an everyday basis. If you think about something that you enjoy doing or get satisfaction from, ask yourself why do I enjoy this particular activity? What makes it meaningful for me? You may well notice a value showing up. Alternatively, you may feel sad or distressed when you think about something you've not done for a while. Exploring this distress is usually a helpful way of identifying something that really matters to you. In other words, look into your pain and see if you can spot whether there's a value that you're feeling distant from. To explore what we mean by this in a bit more detail please take a look at Chris's situation on the next page.

Chris had become increasingly angry with his wife. She had recently been diagnosed with diabetes and, despite her doctor advising her to eat less sugary food, she continued to do so, often hiding what she was eating from Chris. Chris would watch his wife eat more of these 'forbidden' foods and get cross and shout at her. He would nag at her to look after her health more and he persisted in checking up on what she ate each day, which just led to the couple arguing more and more. Chris's greatest fear was that his wife would become ill and that, if she didn't look after herself, he could lose her one day, meaning that they would no longer share their lives and good times together. While exploring his values, Chris realised that there was something within this situation that he cared about deeply and that his current behaviour was not entirely consistent with this value. He realised that behind his anger and upset were some fundamentally important values in relation to his marriage. He valued being fun, caring, supportive and sharing good times with his wife. He began to realise that his wife didn't have to change her behaviour and stop eating sugary food for him to act in accordance with what he valued and cared about most. In fact, once he resolved to 'switch off the autopilot' so that, instead of being driven through life by anger, he was now being more fun, caring and supportive, and was arranging days out to share with his wife, he began to experience his relationship as much more rewarding. When Chris acted on his anger by shouting and nagging his wife, his worst fears were coming true (that he and his wife would no longer enjoy and share good times together). Instead, he chose to act on his values, despite some of the upset he still felt. The added bonus (but not the intention) of doing this was that his wife's mood also improved and she then began to look after her diet and health more.

Another way of looking into your values is to consider them in the context of different areas of your life. Maybe you'd like to think about your values in your own relationships, at work or around your health. Have a go at Exercise 5.5 to consider this in more detail.

## Exercise 5.5
*Values in different life areas*

Another way to clarify your values is to consider a number of different areas of your life. We've suggested some areas of life for you to consider what your values are in each of these important areas (you might find it helpful to use your list of important values from Exercise 5.4 to help you with this).

| Area of life | What kinds of words describe who you want to be in each of these areas? |
| --- | --- |
| Family | |
| Friends | |
| Arts and music | |
| Adversity or difficulties | |
| Spirituality | |

| | |
|---|---|
| Intimate relationships | |
| Work/Study | |
| Societal/Community | |
| Health | |
| Leisure and play | |
| Parenting | |

### Uncovering values through experience

The observer perspective, as usual, is incredibly important at this point.

The observer perspective can help you to notice (and free you up from) the stories your mind generates about your values, such as *'I should value this, I should value that'*, and instead take a different perspective, allowing you to tap into your actual lived experience to guide you towards what you value in life. For example, from your observer perspective you can really notice how you feel while doing certain activities. Noticing when you feel the greatest sense of being alive, engaged, or living with a sense of meaning, purpose and/or emotional distress can be a great indicator that there is something of value in what you are doing.

In essence, the observer perspective can be used to find a sense of direction, bypassing our chattering, evaluative minds and allowing us instead to make direct contact with our actual lived experience. So, from our observer perspective we can notice, on a moment-by-moment basis, what we're experiencing, which can help us to identify what matters most to us. If something seems meaningful, we need to notice that! Once we have identified the core ingredients of a meaningful and purposeful life, the observer perspective can help us once again to remain on track and commit to vigorously pursuing our values through what we do, even when our minds try to lead us off track.

The following exercise can sometimes help us to notice (rather than think about) what we value. Give it a go and see what comes up for you. It might be helpful to have a pen and paper or your electronic device at the ready to scribble some notes down.

## Exercise 5.6 🚲
## Your 80th birthday party
### (adapted from Hayes et al. 1999)

We would like you to imagine that somehow you have
travelled forward in time to a particular event. We would like
you to imagine that you are present at your own 80th birthday
party. However strange that may seem, please give it a go. Let's
imagine that you're standing at the back of the room, looking
around and noticing who is there. We'd like you to imagine
that everyone who is important to you has come together to
celebrate your 80th. This includes people who are important
to you now and also people who have been important to you in
the past and who might be important to you in the future.

As you look around noticing who is there, imagine that the
party is nearing its end and it's time for the speeches. Imagine
that somebody who is extremely important to you is getting
up on stage or taking the microphone and beginning to give
a speech – and the speech is all about YOU. The speaker is

talking about the kind of person you are, the way you have lived your life and the impact that you have had on their life. Importantly, the things they are saying are *whatever it is that you would most want to hear them say*. They are not saying what you think they should, or what they might be expected to say – but simply whatever you would most want to hear.

Please focus on that for a little while and imagine what you would most like to hear. Try to tune in to your body and emotions as you hear this person speaking. Perhaps you are moved more strongly by certain things they say than by others, giving you an indication of what matters most to you.

Next, that speech comes to an end and another person who is very important to you takes the microphone or gets up on stage. Once again they start to give a speech, which describes the kind of person you are and the way you have lived your life. As before, imagine hearing them say whatever you would *most want to hear them say*. Please spend a little while reflecting on that, and again tune into noticing what shows up in your body and emotions.

In your own time, when it feels right to bring the exercise to an end please do so, and spend a few minutes thinking through or writing down the kinds of words you noticed most wanting to hear.

How did you find that exercise? Take a few minutes to reflect on whether the things the speakers said were similar to the values you identified within the previous exercises. It may be that you identified different values; on the other hand, they may be exactly the same.

## Getting closer to your values

Once you've created a list of values in life, the next stage is to consider where you would place yourself in relation to each of these values. In other words, are you actually living in accordance with these fundamentally important things? As you reflect on how you have behaved over the last few weeks or months, to what extent did you behave in a manner consistent with these values? Have a go in the next exercise.

## Exercise 5.7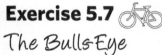

### The Bulls-Eye

(adapted from Lundgren, 2012)

- Allocate each of your values a number – not necessarily in order of importance, but simply as a label.

- Now, see if you can plot each value according to how consistently you are behaving in accordance with that value. For example, if you allocated #1 to 'being loving', plot '1' somewhere on the target on the following page. Plotting a value directly on the centre, i.e. on the bulls-eye, indicates that, as you reflect on your behaviour over the past days, weeks or months, you are entirely satisfied that your behaviour has fully reflected this value. As you plot a value on each concentric circle out from the bulls-eye, this reflects an increasing sense of discrepancy between your behaviour and how you would ideally choose to act.

- Continue plotting each of your values in this manner, until you've done them all. What do you make of your bulls-eye? Are your numbers in or near the bulls-eye or on the outer circles?

- Spend a few moments reflecting on your values. Which are being well served? Which might require a bit of work? Which would be your priority to work on? What would be involved if you committed to doing something to move towards the bulls-eye in any one of these values? What would others actually witness you doing?

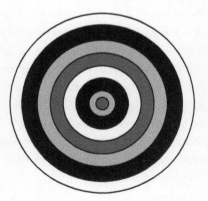

## Losing touch with values

As illustrated in the example at the start of the chapter, in which life was represented by a large glass jar, sometimes when we go through difficult times in life – and particularly when we feel low, angry or anxious – it can be difficult to remain connected to our values. It can be difficult to continue spending time doing things that really matter to us. As a result of efforts to try to control unwanted thoughts and feelings, life can become narrower. It's almost as if so much time, energy and attention has been devoted to trying to get over or beat unwanted thoughts and emotions that there's not much room for anything else. This can happen for a variety of reasons.

- **Distraction and avoidance**: Consider Mark, who distracts himself from worry by playing computer games and subsequently starts to feel disconnected from his family. Sometimes sadder examples of this process can be found in substance misuse. When drugs are used to relieve negative emotional states, people's lives can become narrower, restricted and sometimes entirely focused on finding the next drink or hit – sometimes at the expense of all else.

What's more, in the interests of trying to control 'problems', people may make changes in their lives to avoid unwanted feelings, which can take people away from what matters to them. For example, Steve avoids going to work, drops out of his football club and stops going out at the weekend to avoid the overwhelming sense of anxiety he experiences on public transport. As a result, he no longer sees his friends and seems disconnected from his values, which include being social, healthy and fun.

■ *A drop in self-confidence*: When we are depressed or anxious, the things we used to enjoy can seem hard, and it can become difficult to gain a sense of enjoyment from anything. This leaves us much less inclined to return to doing the things that we used to enjoy or find satisfying, particularly because short-term benefits can often be found in less demanding activities. Sometimes short-term gains can become much more powerful than longer-term rewards, and our behaviour can easily drift away from our values, which can often incur challenge and difficulty in the short term.

When it comes to finding renewed enjoyment in activities, this can often be a bit like planting seeds in a garden. Sometimes a number of seeds need to be planted. Some won't germinate and some will start to grow but won't reach full height. Sooner or later though, a seed will be sown that will grow tall and strong, and bear fruit. In much the same way, people often need to get back to *doing* things. They might not immediately enjoy these activities in the way they used to, and initially they may find them anxiety-provoking, effortful or demanding. But, sooner or later, they might start to experience the old sense of enjoyment, reward or satisfaction again.

- ■ ***Getting stuck in old patterns***: Just like the 'two paths' metaphor at the start of the chapter, it can become very easy to continue taking the well-trodden path rather than waking up and realising the scope for choice in terms of how we respond within challenging situations. For example, Nicole found it very difficult to tolerate even the slightest criticism from her partner. She would become angry and felt compelled to prove him wrong. In time, she became very good at winning any arguments they had. This way of responding became easy and automatic for Nicole and although she got to take a smug 'victory lap' every time she won an argument, it left her feeling empty inside, upset with herself for the way she spoke to her partner and, over time, less loved and disconnected from him.

■ **Procrastination**: Sometimes fear of failing, boredom or other difficult emotions associated with the challenge of doing something important can get in the way of focusing on what we are trying to do. We can often fall into the trap of avoiding these feelings by distracting ourselves away from the task, or by thinking about anything other than what we are actually trying to achieve. This brings a small sense of relief in the short term, but of course leads to enormous frustration in the longer term as the task becomes more and more drawn out and our life becomes defined by less meaningful activities.

## Hitting the bulls-eye

If your bulls-eye from Exercise 5.7 reflects some discrepancy between how you've been behaving recently and how you'd ideally choose to behave, you're certainly not alone! Hopefully, some of the reasons above can help you to understand why this might have occurred. However, the good news is that it is entirely within your control to do things differently. The final section of this chapter will focus on *action*. What will you commit to doing over the coming minutes, hours, days, weeks, months and years that will allow you to move a step closer towards the bulls-eye in relation to any one of your values, no matter how big or small the step? Let's take a look at that right now.

### It's time to take action!

This bit is really straightforward. Enough of the talking, it's time for some action. We can offer you some theoretical ideas regarding what seems to increase the probability of success, but at this stage it really is over to you! What would you be willing to commit to doing in the service of one of your chosen values? What small step could you take to move you closer to what you really care about? Please use the exercise below if it feels helpful to do so!

## Exercise 5.8
*Time for action*

Use the bulls-eye to choose one value you would like to work on (you can go back to choose another to work on later). What would you be willing to commit to *doing* that would move you one step towards the bulls-eye, no matter how big or small the step?

- ■ The value I will be working on is:

  ....................................................................................

- ■ Over the next hour, the action I will commit to doing is:

  ....................................................................................

- ■ Over the next day, the action I will commit to doing is:

  ....................................................................................

- ■ Over the next week, the action I will commit to doing is:

  ....................................................................................

- ■ Over the next month, the action I will commit to doing is:

  ....................................................................................

- ■ Over the next year, the action I will commit to doing is:

  ....................................................................................

As you take committed action towards your values, it is highly likely that you will encounter some undesirable experiences and barriers to your progress. These may involve thoughts (such as *I can't do this*, *I'll do it later*, *I'm too tired or busy right now*) and emotions (such as fear, guilt, shame, frustration, loss, boredom, etc.). It is important to consider the thoughts and feelings that might show up and how you might stay on track when they do so. So, continue this exercise by thinking through the questions below.

What thoughts are likely to show up and could get in the way of my progress?

....................................................................................................................

....................................................................................................................

What feelings are likely to show up and could get in the way of my progress?

....................................................................................................................

....................................................................................................................

What techniques (possibly from the 'Loosen up!' chapter) will I use to respond to these thoughts and feelings when they show up?

..............................................................................................................

..............................................................................................................

On a scale of 1 to 10, how *willing* am I to experience these thoughts and feelings as I pursue what I really care about (1 = not at all willing, 10 = completely and entirely willing)?

............
(Remember, anything less than 10 might not work |so well!)

## Barriers to effective action – what to look out for

There are some tools that seem to make it more likely that people will achieve their goals. We describe some of these tools here – see which ones you can use to increase the likelihood that you will achieve your goals.

### *Well-developed goals*

We've all made New Year resolutions to 'do more exercise', 'go to the gym' or 'have a healthier lifestyle'. One of the reasons these resolutions rarely make it past the second week is that they are not necessarily well-developed goals. Well-developed goals are described by the acronym '**SMART**', which stands for *specific, meaningful, adaptive, realistic* and *time-bound*.

**S** = **a specific** goal - this might be 'I will go to the gym on Mondays, Thursdays and Saturdays for a minimum of 45 minutes' - versus 'I'll go to the gym'.

**M** = **a meaningful** goal - which value is this goal linked to?

**A** = **an adaptive** goal - how will this goal actually enhance your life?

**R** = **a realistic** goal - can you achieve this goal (do you lack any resources, i.e. time, money or facilities, that will make this goal more difficult to achieve)?

**T** = **a time-bound** goal - when exactly will you aim to achieve this by?

*(Harris, 2008)*

### *Beware of emotional goals*

Be careful not to set yourself emotional goals. Emotional goals might sound like *'I'll be happier'*, *'I want to have more self-confidence/ self-esteem'*, *'I'll aim to get rid of these horrible thoughts and feelings and to feel less anxious/sad/guilty'*, etc. By setting emotional goals, aren't we just falling back into the same old trap of trying to exert control over our unwanted psychological experiences? This can lead us off-track once again, particularly if trying to avoid certain emotions leads us to do things that aren't entirely consistent with our values. As we've discussed, often a fulfilling, satisfying and meaningful life comes with emotional pain. A more helpful stance towards this emotional pain is often characterised by a looser, willing and accepting attitude – as we discussed in the 'Loosen up!' chapter.

### *Willingness – plain and simple*

Increasing your willingness to experience unwanted thoughts and feelings can be crucial in taking committed action and living a value-based life. It's our autopilot attempts to control, avoid and eliminate unwanted thoughts and feelings that can sometimes get in the way of us taking committed, value-based action. So it's important that you continue to keep your values in mind (perhaps write them down on a piece of paper or log them on your phone so they can more easily be held in mind) and your willingness level turned up high as you continue to step up. In this way, you can define yourself and your life based on your values and associated action, rather than always being driven through life by your thoughts and feelings.

It is important to remember that there is no such thing as partial willingness. In the 'Loosen up!' chapter we introduced the idea of a 'willingness dial' – this willingness dial needs to be cranked up to its highest level if we're going to stay on track in the presence of very painful thoughts and feelings. Don't forget though, willingness is not about tolerating thoughts and feelings, increasing our willpower or like hanging on for dear life while riding a white-knuckle ride! Instead, willingness involves taking an accepting and curious stance towards our unwanted experiences (using the techniques in the 'Loosen up!' chapter), allowing these thoughts and feelings to come and go *in the interests of continuing vigorously to pursue our values in life.*

### Telling other people

Research has shown that we are more likely to stick to our goals and take action if we make a public announcement about what we intend to do. In essence, making ourselves accountable for our intended actions can increase the likelihood that we follow through on them. With this in mind, you might find it helpful to tell someone you care about – a friend, your partner, family members or a colleague perhaps – about the value-based goals that you are intending to achieve. Alternatively, you can choose to make yourself accountable to yourself by writing your goal on a piece of paper and sticking it where you will be reminded of it – on the fridge door or the bathroom mirror perhaps, or maybe set yourself a recurring reminder in your diary or mobile phone.

### Trying versus doing

*'Try not. Do, or do not. There is no try.'*

– Yoda

As you've seen, this chapter is all about stepping up; to behave boldly in ways that are based on your values, taking along for the ride whatever thoughts and feelings may show up.

A key point to emphasise here is that we are talking about *action*. We (and many others we've met) have often expressed an intention to try to change how we behave in a particular area of our lives. For example, we might *try* to go to the gym more often, or *try* to be more patient at home, or *try* to call distant family members more regularly. Whether trying to do these things will make any difference to our lives is unknown. Let us explain what we mean by this by asking you to take part in Exercise 5.9.

## Exercise 5.9

### Sit down! Stand up!

If you are not sitting down right now then find somewhere to sit. If, for whatever reason, you can't sit down right now then maybe return to this exercise later.

Ok, so now that you are sitting down somewhere, comfortably we hope, we want you to:

**Try to stand up**
If you would, right now please, *try to stand up* ... and once you have done that please continue reading.

So what happened? The chances are that you stood right up, straight away, without much contemplating, delay or *trying* at all. And yet, the instruction was to *try* to stand up, rather than *doing* anything at all. What are the implications of this important but subtle difference?

What's called for when it comes to behavioural change is *doing*. Unfortunately, the truth is that 'trying' in these situations gets us nowhere. It's only action that moves us forward. So the idea is rather than *trying* to act on our values, instead we could just get on and *do something* that is value-based. If we only ever think about our values and/or only *decide* to act on them but never actually *do something* to put them into action, then we will never fully experience their impact in our lives. Even if you take the smallest behavioural step you can imagine towards one of your values, it is likely to make a difference to how you experience life.

That brings us to the end of the chapter. We hope it's given you lots of ideas for how you might continue to clarify what really matters to you and what you really care about in your life. We hope that you are now inspired to begin putting these values into action and truly step up to living a richer, fuller and more meaningful life. In the next and final chapter we hope to *round up* by bringing together the three key aspects of ACT, *wake up*, *loosen up* and *step up*, to help you consider how you can continue to combine these principles throughout your life. We are also keen to leave you with some further ideas and tips for your continued journey of applying ACT to your life. First, here are your summary points from this chapter.

## Chapter 5 summary points

- Rather than automatically being led through life by your thoughts and feelings, you can instead choose to lead your life guided by what matters most to you: your values.

- Values refer to our heart's deepest desires; they are what we would choose our life to be about, the kind of person we want to be, what we want to stand for in particular situations and the personal qualities we ideally wish to demonstrate. Values are the preferred directions we choose to take in life and they can be used to guide our ongoing behaviour and action.

- You can clarify and define your values in many ways. You can consider what is important to you in different areas of your life. Your observer perspective can help you to notice what matters most to you and also help you to stay on track. Remember: where there is pain there are often also values.

- We can lose contact with our values when we use distraction, avoidance and procrastination to control unwanted thoughts and feelings. This often happens when we go through life on autopilot, repeating old patterns of behaviour.

- Alternatively, we can choose to increase our willingness to have undesirable psychological experiences when we take committed action towards a more value-driven life. We can use loosen up techniques to help us respond more effectively to thoughts and feelings in order to stay on track, vigorously pursuing our values.

- Setting SMART goals is a useful way to take action on our values. In the end what makes the difference is *action*.

# 6 Round up

So that's it (well, almost anyway)! We do hope you've enjoyed this introduction to the ACT model and we hope this book has offered you some useful ideas. We've covered a lot of ground (as much as we could squeeze in!), so we would like to use this final chapter to **round up** everything we've covered and to offer you some suggestions regarding how to continue to practise applying ACT in your everyday life. As with any new skill, now you're familiar with the basic techniques, the most important thing to do next is practise!

## Keeping flexible

Before we offer you a few further tips and tools, we want to summarise how the main ideas and techniques covered in this book all come together.

Although we have introduced the key ideas of ACT (*wake up*, *loosen up* and *step up*) in a consecutive fashion, we hope that we've explained clearly how these core processes tend to interact and influence each other in any given moment, rather than working in isolation. In this way, they help us to cultivate greater *psychological flexibility*. That is, they help us to respond more effectively to the thoughts and feelings we might otherwise struggle with, fully and without defence, in a manner that allows us *actively* to move towards living the kind of life we really care about and being the kind of person we truly want to be.

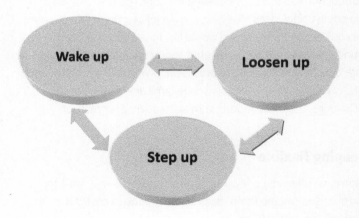

To illustrate how the main ideas of ACT interact with one another we'd like to return to Lisa, who we first introduced you to in Chapter 1. As you may recall, Lisa had begun to struggle with anxiety following a difficult break-up with her partner. As her anxiety tended to increase when socialising, as well as when speaking up in meetings at work, she quite understandably began to avoid these anxiety-provoking situations. She found herself staying at home alone more often, distracting herself with TV, and had also begun to rely on alcohol to help get her through social events. Her struggles with anxiety left her feeling fed up and she did not recognise herself any more. Here's how some of the ideas and techniques of wake up, loosen up and step up worked together to help Lisa to become more 'flexible' and get unstuck.

By practising present moment awareness (wake up), Lisa became aware of her tendency to avoid experiencing anxiety and how her autopilot tendencies to worry, screen her calls from friends and excuse herself from meetings at work all shared this common purpose (loosen up). She noticed (wake up) how her worry and avoidance of anxiety made her anxiety worse in the long run and how she felt increasingly low as she moved away from what she really cared about in life (step up). She practised being willing to experience these painful emotions (loosen up), learning to observe them through mindfulness exercises (wake up). As she began to free herself from the trap of struggling with her unwanted feelings (loosen up) she was then better able to notice (wake up) how these feelings were providing her with important clues about what really mattered to her in life and what sort of person she truly wanted to be (step up).

For example, she realised that looking after her physical and mental health, having fun and connecting with friends, as well as being a supportive and proactive colleague at work, mattered a great deal to her, and how drinking alcohol, staying indoors and skipping meetings were not working well for her. Lisa devised an action plan around some value-based goals and committed to this plan. She decided that over the coming week she would call her closest friend to arrange a time for them to meet for a coffee. The following week, she would meet a larger group of friends for a night out. She decided that she would not drink any alcohol. She also decided to attend one work meeting each week.

As she pursued her values (step up), she continued to practise present moment awareness and mindfulness exercises along the way (wake up). These exercises helped her to notice when her mind tried to pull her off track with unhelpful thoughts. When Lisa found herself in challenging situations (step up) she employed various techniques (loosen up) which helped her to carry on doing things in accordance with her values and not let her thoughts (for instance, *'I can't do this, I'm too anxious'*; *'I'm boring and everyone will find me uninteresting'*; *'I need a drink'*) and any unwanted feelings (e.g. anxiety, tiredness, sadness, urges to drink) take her off track.

So, how about you? Like Lisa, are you also ready to increase your psychological flexibility and become unstuck? Or, to put this a different way, consider your answer to the following question:

*Given the distinction between YOU and the thoughts and feelings you are struggling with (wake up), are you willing to experience these unwanted thoughts and feelings fully without defence, as they are, not as they say they are (loosen up) while you do the things that move you towards what you really care about (step up), in this situation, right now (wake up)?*

If your answer to the question above is 'Yes', then great! It's time to get practising.

It is really important that you continue to practise the techniques in this book (and others) if you want to enhance your psychological flexibility. We would encourage you to practise them regularly, not just at times when you may be going through a rough patch.

We understand that life is busy and it is very tempting to forget to practise these techniques when life seems to be going well. At these times we tend to assume that there isn't any need to take care of ourselves or engage in strategies for self-help. However, these tend to be some of the most important times to be practising these techniques if you value psychological health and wellbeing. By committing to regularly practising the principles and tools of ACT, regardless of how you feel, you're likely to experience a greater sense of satisfaction and well-being in life.

## The choice is yours

Throughout this book, we have been exploring how we can switch off our psychological autopilot mode so that, instead of being driven through life by our thoughts, emotions and physical sensations, we can *choose* what to do according to what matters to us most. This issue of choice is absolutely central in ACT. Everything you have read about, all the strategies and techniques you have experimented with, have all been orientated towards maximising the scope for you to choose to behave in a manner consistent with the kind of person you want to be and the kind of life you want to have.

At almost every moment, we have a choice regarding how we act. At each of these moments, we can choose to *DO* something that either moves us towards or away from our values. To return to the 'fork in the path' metaphor that we started the three previous chapters with, at each of these moments you can *choose* between the first or the second path. The choices we make can have a profound impact on the course of our lives.

## It's your choice

One way is the route you've taken on many occasions in the past and is a well-worn track. It's reasonably clear with no significant obstacles and you know where it takes you. If you were cycling on autopilot, you would automatically turn down this path without hesitation. The second track is overgrown, thick with brambles and full of potholes. You've never taken this path before and it looks like a difficult, menacing and arduous route, yet it leads you to everything that you care deeply about in life. Which path would you choose?

This issue of 'choice' is so important that you can use this word as an acronym to remember many of the important ideas ACT has to offer. Every time you encounter a challenge in life you can make a **CHOICE** ......

**C = Contact** the present moment to wake up to your struggles with internal experiences

**H = Hold** any unwanted thoughts, emotions and sensations lightly

**O = Observe** these internal experiences, as they pass through you, and loosen up around them

**I = Identify** what matters most to you

**C = Clarify** where you want to go and what actions will take you there

**E = Engage** in value-driven, committed action and step up

This brief acronym includes some really important ideas that by now you'll be familiar with. We suggest you use this acronym each time you have a choice to make within a challenging emotional situation. Life offers many opportunities to expose yourself to difficult situations that might elicit unwanted emotions, thoughts and sensations. The way in which you respond to these psychological experiences can move you either towards or away from your values.

## Showing up in life

Exposing oneself to emotionally challenging situations is probably the single most effective way of enriching our lives. Continuing to take these bold moves and 'show up' in your life while responding to your thoughts and feelings in a helpful manner is a sure-fire way of living a full, meaningful and purposeful existence. Take opportunities to step forward into these situations that present a challenge to you while purposely and actively setting yourself other value-based goals. Approach these challenges boldly, armed with the tools that you have found useful in this book; remember you don't have to *feel* 100% willing to do so, you just have to *be* 100% willing. Even with the powerful tools of ACT by your side you may still not *feel* completely ready or confident to take on these emotionally challenging scenarios, which is understandable, absolutely fine and certainly *not* a reason to avoid them! The rating form below can help you to keep track of how you do within these situations. You may find it helpful to work through this form as and when you choose to put yourself into these challenging and life-enhancing situations.

## Exercise 6.1
### Approaching challenging situations

**Control**: How much effort are you putting into trying to push away difficult thoughts and/or avoid unwanted emotions?

**Willingness**: How open and accepting are you towards these thoughts and emotions?

**Valued action**: How much are you engaging in behaviour that is consistent with your values and goals?

**Helpfulness**: In response to emotionally challenging situations, how helpful are these levels of control, willingness and valued action in terms of moving you towards the life you want?

| Challenging Situation: | Control 0–10 | Willingness 0–10 | Valued action 0–10 | Helpfulness 0–10 |
|---|---|---|---|---|
| | | | | |
| | | | | |
| | | | | |

## Holding your values in mind

As you know all too well by now, ACT does not aim to reduce the unwanted psychological experiences we encounter in life, such as anxiety, fear, sadness or anger. Research tells us that it's not the absence of these experiences, regardless of how uncomfortable they may be, that actually brings us a sense of fulfilment and satisfaction in life. Instead, what brings a greater sense of wellbeing and meaning into our lives is when we take active steps towards living a more value-driven life.

Clearly, values are an enormously important part of the ACT model. Once you've worked your way through a book like this, spent time identifying and clarifying your values in life and perhaps things are better, it can be tempting to put these values in a box and store them in a cupboard, with the intention to get them out again next time you need them. The difficulty with this approach is that they can often become buried under other stored items in the cupboard and become difficult to hold in mind.

For this reason, we recommend keeping your values in an easily accessible place: in your wallet, on your phone, in your diary, on the front of the fridge. Keep them somewhere that allows you to hold them in mind. What's more, values change! They are dynamic and they often change as we grow older or take on different roles in life. It can be helpful to review your values regularly and to consider, perhaps on a weekly or monthly basis, the extent to which your behaviour has been in accordance with these values. Remember, a central question in ACT is whether any action you take represents a move towards or away from the person you want to be and the life you want to lead, so you'll need your values in mind as you continue to make these CHOICES!

## What would a 'relapse' look like?

What is a relapse? When you hear the word 'relapse', what does that mean to you? Often, we think of relapses as they pertain to drug or alcohol abuse. Someone who 'relapses' might return to using a substance following a period of abstinence. When we are focusing on thoughts and emotions, however, what do we mean by relapse?

A relapse from an ACT perspective is certainly not an increase in difficult or unwanted thoughts, emotions or physical sensations. We know that emotions, sensations and thoughts might increase or decrease in a way that is often not under our control.

From an ACT perspective, a relapse occurs when someone begins to deviate away from orientating their behaviour around their values. Of course, this happens to us all on a regular basis, so perhaps a better word rather than 'relapse' is 'setback'. Setbacks are an entirely normal part of human life, no matter how much progress you've made towards your goals and values and no matter how hard you try. Perhaps, therefore, what's important isn't necessarily whether these setbacks occur, but instead how you respond to them when they do.

Getting back on track following a setback would involve utilising some of the exact same skills that you might use to manage any other emotionally challenging situation. In other words, wake up to the life-narrowing, autopilot struggles with unwanted thoughts and feelings that are holding you back; use the loosen up techniques to manage these thoughts and emotions around your setback more effectively; and then step up to taking value-driven action that will get you back on track once again.

## How to make best use of this book in the future

In terms of using this book from now on, we recommend spending a few weeks practising some of the tools and techniques you've read about before returning to the book to remind yourself of others. Hopefully, with this approach, you'll explore and discover what works for you and develop a 'tool box' of effective strategies. It goes without saying that different things work for different people and in different situations, too; so you'll probably discover what works for you, and when, through a process of trial and error. When a tool or strategy moves you towards the kind of person you want to be or towards the kind of life you want to live, keep using it! When a tool or strategy doesn't work in this way, discard it and try another.

Inevitably, this book represents only a very brief introduction to some very important ideas. That said, we do hope that you will continue to revisit it from time to time to remind yourself of these ideas and to ensure you stay on track!

In the next section we have included a list of other ACT resources for anyone who is keen to find out more about what ACT has to offer, such as popular books, websites, apps and a range of other resources, including links to ACT therapy/coaching services. We urge you to remember that ACT isn't just an approach for helping people who are struggling with psychological difficulties, it is also a model for 'better living' more generally; it's not just for those of us who are going through a difficult time. ACT offers us all a set of 'life skills' which have the potential to be enormously helpful for each and every one of us.

## Goodbye

All that is left to say now is 'Goodbye'. Thank you for choosing this book. We sincerely hope that reading it has been a useful experience for you and, whatever your reasons were for choosing it, we hope that it offered you what you were looking for. We really believe in ACT and we hope that you can also see its potential to help you and other people too.

If you share our appreciation of these ideas, we urge you to get them out there! Tell your family and friends about what this model has to offer. Share the resources listed in the appendix with people at work, school, in the pub and in the gym. Talk about it with people you meet. While we appreciate that ACT isn't for everyone (unfortunately there isn't a model that seems to work for everyone just yet!), you would be amazed at how many people could benefit.

From us both, we sincerely wish you well on your journey ahead, as you continue to *wake up*, *loosen up* and *step up*!

> *'We have only begun to imagine the fullness of life.'*
> *– Denise Levertov*

# Recommended reading

Ciarrochi, J., Hayes, L., & Bailey, A. (2012). *Get Out of Your Mind and Into your Life for Teens: A Guide to Living an Extraordinary Life.* New Harbinger

Ciarrochi, J., Bailey, A., & Harris, R. (2015). *The Weight Escape: Stop Fad Dieting, Start Losing Weight and Reshape Your Life Using Cutting-Edge Psychology.* Robinson

Dahl, J. C., & Lundgren, T. (2006). *Living Beyond Your Pain: Using Acceptance and Commitment Therapy to Ease Chronic Pain.* New Harbinger

DuFrene, T., & Wilson, K. G. (2012). *The Wisdom to Know the Difference: An Acceptance and Commitment Therapy Workbook for Overcoming Substance Abuse.* New Harbinger

Eifert, G. H., McKay, M., & Forsyth, J. P. (2006). *ACT on Life Not on Anger: The New Acceptance and Commitment Therapy Guide to Problem Anger*. New Harbinger

Eifert, G. H., & Forsyth, J. P. (2008). *The Mindfulness and Acceptance Workbook for Anxiety: A Guide to Breaking Free from Anxiety, Phobias and Worry*. New Harbinger.
Please see the link below for details of a research study that tested the effectiveness of this self-help book:
www.drjohnforsyth.com/johns-blog/is-self-help-helpful-a-look-at-the-mindfulness-acceptance-workbook-for-anxiety

Ferreira, N., & Gillanders, D. T. (2015). *Better Living with IBS: A Step-by-Step Programme to Managing your Symptoms So You Can Enjoy Living Life to the Full!* Exisle Publishing

Follette, V. V., & Pistorello, J. (2007). *Finding Life beyond Trauma: Using Acceptance and Commitment Therapy to Heal from Post-Traumatic Stress and Trauma-Related Problem*. New Harbinger

Harris, R. (2008). *The Happiness Trap: How to Stop Struggling and Start Living*. Robinson

Harris, R. (2009). *ACT with Love: Stop Struggling, Reconcile Differences and Strengthen Your Relationship with Acceptance and Commitment Therapy*. New Harbinger Publications

Harris, R. (2011). *The Confidence Gap: From Fear to Freedom*. Robinson

Harris, R. (2011). *The Reality Slap: How to Find Fulfilment when Life Hurts*. Robinson

Hayes, S. C., & Smith, S. (2005). *Get out of your Mind and into your Life: The New Acceptance and Commitment Therapy*. New Harbinger

Lejeune, C. (2007). *The Worry Trap. How to Free Yourself from Worry and Anxiety Using Acceptance and Commitment Therapy*. New Harbinger

McCurry, C. (2009). *Parenting Your Anxious Child with Mindfulness and Acceptance: A Powerful New Approach to Overcoming Fear, Panic and Worry using Acceptance and Commitment Therapy*. New Harbinger

Meadows, G. (2014). *The Sleep Book: How to Sleep Well Every Night*. Orion

Oliver, J., Hill, J., & Morris, E. (2015). *ACTivate Your Life: Using Acceptance and Mindfulness to Build a Life that is Rich, Fulfilling and Fun*. Robinson (includes chapters specifically focusing on depression, anxiety, anger and self-esteem)

Owen, R. (2013). *Living with the Enemy: Coping with the Stress of Chronic Illness Using CBT, Mindfulness and Acceptance*. Routledge

Robinson, P. J., & Strosahl, K. D. (2008). *The Mindfulness and Acceptance Workbook for Depression: Using Acceptance and Commitment Therapy to Move Through Depression and Create a Life Worth Living*. New Harbinger

Sandoz, E. K., & Wilson, K. G. (2011). *The Mindfulness and Acceptance Workbook for Bulimia: A Guide to Breaking Free from Bulimia Using Acceptance and Commitment Therapy*. New Harbinger

Sinclair, M., & Seydel, J. (2013). *Mindfulness for Busy People: Turning from Frantic and Frazzled into Calm and Composed*. Pearson

Sinclair, M., & Seydel, J. (2016). *Working with Mindfulness: Keeping Calm and Focused to Get the Job Done*. Pearson

Walser, R. D., & Westrup, D. (2009). *The Mindful Couple: How Acceptance and Mindfulness Can Lead You to the Life You Want*. New Harbinger

Williams, M., & Penman, D. (2011). *Mindfulness: A Practical Guide to Finding Peace in a Frantic World*. Piaktus

Wilson, K. G., & DuFrene, T. (2010). *Things Might Go Terribly, Horribly Wrong: A Guide to Life Liberated from Anxiety*. New Harbinger

# Further useful resources

## Websites about ACT

- The Association for Contextual Behavioural Science (ACBS):
  https://contextualscience.org/act_for_the_public

- The Happiness Trap:
  www.thehappinesstrap.com/about_act

- ACT Mindfully:
  www.actmindfully.com.au

- Working with ACT:
  http://workingwithact.com

- The Career Psychologist:
  www.thecareerpsychologist.com

## ACT-based apps

- ACT Companion: The Happiness Trap App – a great resource for ACT-based exercises and pre-recorded mindfulness audio files

## Academic and research papers

- A-Tjak, J. G., Davis, M. L., Morina, N., Powers, M. B., Smits, J. A., & Emmelkamp, P. M. (2015). A meta-analysis of the efficacy of acceptance and commitment therapy for clinically relevant mental and physical health problems. *Psychotherapy and Psychosomatics, 84*(30), 30–36

- Please see the ACBS website for a full list of published meta-analyses and Randomised Controlled Trials: https://contextualscience.org/state_of_the_act_evidence

## How to find ACT therapists

- ACBS – This is a list of therapists who identify themselves as ACT therapists and are available for consultation, globally: https://contextualscience.org/civicrm/ profile?gid=17&reset=1&force=1

- The Brisbane ACT Centre: www.brisbaneactcentre.com.au

- City Psychology Group, London:
  www.citypsychology.com

- Contextual Consulting, London:
  https://contextualconsulting.co.uk

## ACT-related videos

- Steven Hayes' (founder of ACT) TEDx Talk – Psychological
  flexibility: How love turns pain into purpose:
  www.youtube.com/watch?v=o79_gmO5ppg

- Steven Hayes' (founder of ACT) TEDx Talk – Mental Brakes
  to Avoid Mental Breaks:
  www.youtube.com/watch?v=GnSHpBRLJrQ

- Jonathan Bricker TEDx Talk on ACT applied to smoking
  cessation – The secret of self control:
  www.youtube.com/watch?v=tTb3d5cjSFl

- The Career Psychologist – Headstuck! What is Experiential
  Avoidance (Rob Archer):
  www.youtube.com/watch?v=C-ZuqeyxULM

- Russ Harris – Values vs Goals (animation):
  www.youtube.com/watch?v=T-IRbuy4XtA

- Russ Harris – The Struggle Switch (animation):
  www.youtube.com/watch?v=rCp1l16GCXI

- Joe Oliver – Passengers on the Bus – an Acceptance & Commitment Therapy Metaphor (animation): www.youtube.com/watch?v=Z29ptSuoWRc

- Joe Oliver – The Unwelcome Party Guest – an Acceptance & Commitment Therapy Metaphor (animation): www.youtube.com/watch?v=VYht-guymF4

## Other ACT-related articles

- Steven Hayes' articles on the Huffington Post: www.huffingtonpost.com/steven-c-hayes-phd

- Steven Hayes' articles from Psychology Today: www.psychologytoday.com/blog/get-out-your-mind

- TIME Magazine article: http://content.time.com/time/magazine/article/0,9171,1156613,00.html?cnn=yes

- Michael Sinclair's blog on the Huffington Post: www.huffingtonpost.co.uk/dr-michael-sinclair/how-to-behave-to-the-life-you-want_b_6730226.html

- Kelly Wilson's articles from Psychology Today: www.psychologytoday.com/blog/living-one-life